BOLTON-LE-SANDS

PORTRAIT OF A VILLAGE

BOLTON-LE-SANDS
PORTRAIT OF A VILLAGE

BARRY & LESLEY GUISE

KEITH BUDDEN

ISBN: 978-1-874181-96-5

Published on behalf of the authors by
Scotforth Books, Lancaster
www.scotforthbooks.com
www.carnegiepublishing.com

Printed by Short Run Press Ltd

Contents

Acknowledgements

A book such as this could not have been produced without the help and co-operation of many people. The authors would like to express their gratitude to those individuals who have shared their memories of Bolton-le-Sands and/or have lent photographs and postcards.

Particular thanks go to Dorothy Nelson, who was a mine of information, and to Tony Barker, Maureen Bennnett, Jonathan Clarke, Betty Cottam, Brian Davies, Colin & Margaret Everett, Emmeline Garnett, Nancy Goodrich, Dennis Hough, Kathleen Hill, Henry Millner, Sheila Modley, Marian Rigg, Geoff Shingler, Russell Smith, Jean Turner, Sue Whiteside and Ken Woods.

We are also grateful to Neil Marshall of Burnley Central Library and to Edward Ratcliffe of the Children's Society who provided background information about Burnley Camp School and the Victoria Home for Girls respectively.

Special thanks are due to Kenneth Entwistle who generously allowed the authors to draw on material from his book *From Bodeltone to Bolton-le-Sands*, a detailed history of the village which, sadly, is long out of print.

Last but not least, our thanks to everyone at Carnegie Publishing whose expertise and professionalism are second to none.

Authors

Barry and Lesley Guise are relative newcomers to Bolton-le-Sands having lived in the village for only 36 years. Both are retired teachers, Barry from St Martin's College, Lancaster and Lesley from Lancaster Girls' Grammar School. When not writing books they are often to be found on the local bowling green.

Keith Budden was brought up in Bolton-le-Sands and is well known to most people in the village through his roles as Parish Councillor and District Councillor. In 2008/9 he served as Mayor of the City of Lancaster. One of Keith's many interests is searching out old postcards of Bolton-le-Sands to add to his extensive collection.

Ulverston •

Flookburgh

• Barrow-in-Furness

MORECAMBE
BAY

'Bolton is a large, well-built, and highly respectable village, pleasantly situated on the great north road from Lancaster, four miles north from that town. Here are several genteel residences, some extensive malting establishments, and three respectable inns, and the village is skirted by the Lancaster and Kendal Canal. The church stands on the south side of the village, in view of Morecambe bay. The Free Grammar School was founded in 1625, by Thomas Assheton. There is also at Bolton an Industrial Girls School, erected by subscription in 1840. The addition le-Sands arises from its vicinity to the sands of Morecambe bay, which, at the recession of the tide, becomes a vast plain of sand, intersected by variable channels of fresh water streams.'

Bulmer's Directory 1851

River Kent

Milnthorpe

A6

Grange-over-Sands

Lancaster
Canal

Carnforth

Bolton-le-Sands

River Lune

Morecambe

Lancaster

M6

2 miles

5 kilometres

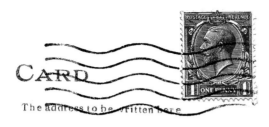

Introduction

While some of the illustrations in this book are old photographs, the majority are early picture postcards mostly dating from the first third of the 20th century. Before telephones became widely available the postcard provided a means of cheap and near-instant communication – the phone call or text message of its day. The postal service at the time was efficient and reliable and next-day delivery was taken for granted. In practice, postcards sent in the morning were often delivered the same day if distances were not too great.

Although plain postcards had been in use in Britain since 1870 as a way of sending non-confidential messages, little thought had been given to the inclusion of pictures. It was not until the end of the century that the Post Office, which controlled such things, sanctioned illustrations to appear on postcards. However, senders were not permitted to write on the same side as the address and any words had to be fitted around the picture on the front of the card. This edict was relaxed in 1902 with the introduction of the 'divided back' – half for the address and half for the message – which freed up the whole of the front of the card for a picture. From then on postcards exploded in popularity and quickly became the standard medium for transmitting short messages. Their simple convenience ensured their success and millions went through the postal service every week.

One reason for the early appeal of the postcard was the small demand it placed on the writer when formal education, for most people, was over by the age of fourteen. While a letter seemed to require a certain formality and correct layout that might daunt the untrained, almost everyone could manage a few words on a postcard. Most messages were perfectly understandable despite eccentric spelling and wayward grammar, often carrying on without recourse to niceties such as capital letters, commas or full stops! Generally, their content tended to adhere to certain standard elements (not much changed today): the greeting, the weather, health of writer, enquiry as to health of correspondent, signing off. These often formed a basis for permutation or variation such as making arrangements for visits, sending and receiving parcels, announcements of births or bereavements, congratulations on birthdays and anniversaries, etc. Some examples are shown overleaf.

Postcards were affordable, could be used by all classes and had the added bonus of a pleasant and interesting picture. By the end of the First World War, however, the craze was over and the number of postcards sent dropped dramatically, not helped by the doubling of the cost of a stamp from ½d to 1d (then to 1½d in 1921) and the more widespread use of the telephone. Postcards still continued to be sent in large numbers through the ensuing decades but never in the same quantities as in the so-called 'Golden Age'.

For its size, Bolton-le-Sands was well documented by local and national photographers, possibly because of its popularity as a holiday destination from late Victorian times. The wide range of postcards that were produced open a window onto an earlier world. They provide a visual record of the changes that have taken place from more than a century ago – of buildings gone or altered, vehicles now obsolete and fashions no longer in vogue – in effect, a pictorial social history of a village.

'Pleased you like your new county. Can you recognise any one on this card? It is a snapshot taken unawares but if your old favourite mare was turned the other way you would know her.'

Xmas Greetings

MAIN RD. BOLTON-LE-SANDS.

This particular scene at the bottom of Packet Hill was carefully chosen to send Christmas greetings in 1916 to an ex-villager who had recently moved to Cornwall.

Townend Bridge, Bolton-le-Sands.

Posted to Great Harwood in 1924, the writer filled the back of this card of the old Town End Bridge with a stream of consciousness, its flow uninterrupted by a single punctuation mark. With a little effort on the part of the reader it does actually make sense: *'Dear Mother and Father just a few lines to say we are enjoying ourselves fine it as been very nice but it is raining we are going to Windermere tomorrow thursday if it fine for the day have you been anywhere write me a card I have a card from Mary they did not say how they liked their digs if the weather keeps nice we might stay till sunday night remember me to Harry with love from Anne'.*

BOLTON – LE –SANDS

Punctuation was also largely absent from this card of Crosshill which accompanied a parcel sent to Bolton in 1916: *'Thursday a dull morning and just received your card pleased all is well. Am sending a parcel of fish by this post they were in the sea this morning just going to post Love to all.'*

An elegantly dressed lady waits for a friend at the entrance gateway to Croftlands, a large house which stood at the junction of Mill Lane and Main Road. The postcard made from this photograph was sent to Liverpool in 1904 to wish the recipient *'Many happy returns of the day and hope you will have a good time'.*

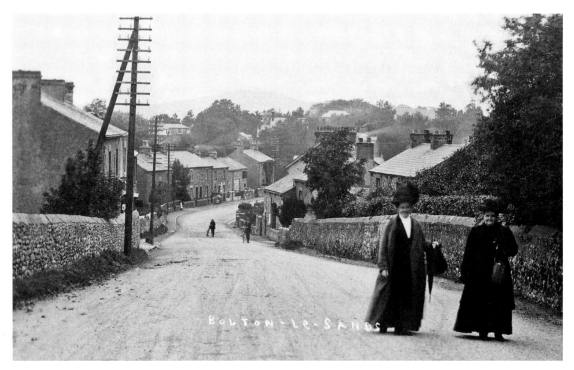

The reliability of same-day postal delivery meant that orders for goods could be placed at the last minute with confidence, as in this card of ladies on Packet Hill sent in 1909 to Mr T. Speight, Fruit and Potato Dealer at 1, Ffrances Passage, Lancaster: *'Dear Sir, Please bring three loads of potatoes tomorrow Wednesday and oblige. Mrs Wilson, Grocer, Bolton-le-Sands.'*

One of the attractions of early postcards is their immediacy. Here a local photographer has gone to the scene of a motoring accident in the village and snapped it for its curiosity value. In March 1922 a lorry crossing Packet Bridge swerved to avoid an oncoming motorcycle and sidecar and crashed through a wall, falling some twenty feet into the garden of John Speight of Bridge House. The lorry also knocked over a pram containing a small child who was thrown out but escaped serious injury, as did the driver of the lorry.

BOLTON LE SANDS

Probably the majority of postcards of Bolton-le-Sands were sent to relatives and friends from people on holiday in the village. This card of a young lady posing for the camera before boarding a coach outside the Packet Boat Hotel was posted to Stockport in September 1910. Ada was writing home to her mother to tell her that *'It has been lovely and fine today and we have been on the shore. We have got nearly 3lb of mushrooms and a lot of blackberries. We will get some to bring home with us.'*

'It has been lovely and fine today and we have been on the shore. We have got nearly 3lb of mushrooms and a lot of blackberries. We will get some to bring home with us.'

Another example was a card sent to Leeds in 1914 from Eddie who was staying with his aunt (and obviously didn't want to waste a minute of his holiday!) *'Got up this morning at 6.20 and had finished breakfast before 7.15 and went out for a walk. I landed at Hest Bank and walked across the sands to Morecambe. Very nice place but not many people astir. Some fine Express trains pass through here. Beautiful weather.'*

The cheapness and easy availability of picture postcards appealed to collectors of all ages and classes and many cards found their way into albums without ever having passed through the postal system. Several appear in this book. The absence of a stamp and postmark means that the precise dating of such cards is not always possible.

A brief history of Bolton-le-Sands

Bolton-le-Sands has, of course, a much longer history than that of the postcard. We know a small settlement called Bodeltone, belonging to the manor of Halton, was in existence before the Norman Conquest as it is recorded in the Domesday Survey. However, it may be assumed that earlier inhabitants of the area were similar to many other small groups, subsisting on fish, shellfish and wildfowl on the margins of Morecambe Bay and practising the rudiments of agriculture on the higher ground inland. The arrival of the Romans in the 1st century AD left a lasting legacy in Lancaster and the Lune Valley and it would be reasonable to believe that their influence spread to this village, but there is no evidence and it could be that the marsh and its people were both equally unattractive and largely ignored.

A later incursion by Anglian peoples in the 5th and 6th centuries left a greater impression on the village, developing its fishing and farming structure and giving it its name. Bodeltone, like numerous other Boltons nationwide, derives from the Old English word *botl* or *bothl* meaning *dwelling* and the ending *tun* meaning *farm* or *village*, ie a very prosaic name for a settlement. Norse invaders arrived in the 10th century via Scotland, Ireland and the Isle of Man. They too settled into the fishing and farming lifestyle and left some of their language among the local placenames, eg *thwaite* from *thveit* for a *piece of land* and *Hawkshead* from *Hawkr,* a personal name and *head* meaning *hill*. They also left more solid evidence of their presence in the form of stone monuments which were found in the parish churchyard. Unfortunately, overenthusiastic clearing and renovation of the church in the 19th century led to their destruction and only fragments remain.

At the time of the Domesday Survey, completed in 1086, Bodeltone was a small village or township, with a church dedicated to St Michael, in a relatively backward part of England. It was assessed for tax purposes as having four carucates of land where one carucate was the amount of ploughland that could be tilled by an 8-ox plough in a year, giving an approximate area of somewhere between 130 and 230 hectares. Little would have changed for the villagers at this time apart from the destination of their taxes; in the space of four years the Manor of Halton, including Bodeltone, changed hands from Tostig (the rebel brother of Harold Godwinson, killed at Stamford Bridge in 1066) to Harold (killed at Hastings in 1066) to William the Conqueror who, in 1070, granted it to one of his main supporters, Roger of Poitou.

Until the 13th century the township of Bodeltone included Slyne with Hest, the Kellets and the hamlet of Stapleton Terne, a small settlement on the south-eastern side of the village. Two of Stapleton's inhabitants retired to Furness Abbey and gave their land to the monastic order. It was developed as a grange or farm for the abbey's monks (roughly where Beaumont Grange is

Remnants of 10th century stone carvings, now kept in the base of Holy Trinity Church tower.

today). When King John visited the area in the early 13th century, he declared that the land was insufficient for the monks' needs and promptly gave them the remainder of Stapleton Terne. The inhabitants either moved to work on the monks' grange or to other parts of the parish and the hamlet decayed so that no trace can be seen today.

The Bolton (or Boulton) of the Middle Ages continued in the fashion of many other villages in the area, with subsistence farming, fishing and wildfowling. Crops such as oats, barley, beans and peas were grown on the partly enclosed croftlands and there is evidence that a watermill, used to grind some of the produce, was in existence at this time. The wetter, low lying fields were good for the growing of flax so that flax processing and linen manufacture became an important part of the village economy. Fishing was mainly for shellfish or flatfish caught by nets fixed on the sands and collected at low tide. Life for the villagers could be hard; poor weather in the early 14th century resulted in famine and this was closely followed by incursions of raiding Scots as much of Northern England was disputed between the English and Scottish thrones. The mid 14th century saw, perhaps, up to one third of the population of Bolton killed by the Black Death.

One factor which gave Bolton a slightly greater importance than its neighbours was its position as the starting point for the route across the sands of Morecambe Bay to Grange and Furness, relevant to the village because of its strong links with Furness Abbey. The numerous records of drownings of fishermen and travellers in local parish registers bear witness to the dangers of the crossing and in the Middle Ages a small chapel or altar existed, probably near what is now St Nicholas Lane where the route started, for prayers or thanks for a safe journey.

Although on another major routeway (the main village street was for many centuries part of the Great North Road, whose path can be traced in Town End and over Thwaite Brow) most traffic was between neighbouring villages with the tracks kept in repair by the manor and abbeys. Some of these developed into the present-day road pattern while others have remained as tracks, eg Mount Pleasant crossroads to Carnforth, or degenerated into minor footpaths, eg St Nicholas Lane to Crag Bank.

The structure of Holy Trinity Church tower remains basically 15th century with later additions such as the clock and stained-glass window.

Tower.
Bolton-le-Sands Parish Church.

By 1500 the parish church had a recognisable stone tower much as we see it today; a bell which hung in the tower in the late 15th century still remains although others have been recast. After Henry VIII's break with Rome and the dissolution of many monasteries, the land and tithes belonging to the abbeys were reassigned, eg Bolton tithes were granted by Henry to Lord Monteagle of Hornby and later to the crown itself in the shape of

Elizabeth I. The tithes were stored in a large barn adjacent to the church, finally dispensed with in the 19th century when tithes were replaced by rents in cash.

Through the 17th century many of the larger and more important buildings in Bolton were constructed of stone; a walk through the village will reveal several datestones from this period. Gradually, over the succeeding centuries, the old timber houses, so susceptible to fire and decay, were replaced by more permanent stone structures and the settlement started to take on the appearance with which we are familiar. The building of the Free Grammar School in 1637, giving the opportunity to study Latin and Greek, enhanced the reputation of the village. In the following century English and arithmetic were added to the curriculum but, unlike the Classics, could be studied only on payment of a fee. At this time, when Lancaster's trans-Atlantic trade was at its height, boys from the West Indies and 'other distant ports' boarded in Bolton and were educated at the school.

During the English Civil War there was a strong Nonconformist element in the parish as church and village sided with the Parliamentarians. The restoration of the monarchy in 1660 brought about a downturn in the fortunes of the church and the incumbents, deprived of some of their living, found it difficult to make ends meet; numerous vicars continued to struggle until the mid 19th century when payment was received instead of tithes, some even suffering the indignity of imprisonment for debt. Although there were no proper records of the number of inhabitants of the village before the 1801 National Census, an assessment for tax purposes in the 1660s recorded 66 households; with an estimated mean number of 5.5 persons per household this suggests a population of around 360. Farming was still the major occupation with sheep becoming increasingly important. The sheep grazed the saltmarsh and their manure, along with seaweed, was highly prized as fertiliser for the arable fields.

The 18th-century village inn, such as the Blue Anchor and the Black Bull, as well as providing food and drink for villagers and travellers alike, became a centre of commerce where deals were struck and meetings and auctions were held. Increased travel at this time meant that the main roads became barely fit for purpose and, despite rates and taxes levied, could not be adequately repaired by the locals held responsible. The solution to this was the introduction of Turnpike Trusts which financed roadworks by collecting tolls from road users. An act of 1751 set up the 'Garstang and Heiring Syke Turnpike Trust' to widen, improve and repair the road from Preston to Lancaster and through 'Slyne, Bolton by the Sands, Carnforth ... Dalton ... a Place called Heiring Syke that divides the Counties of Lancaster and Westmorland'. This enabled the road through Town End, past the church and the

The Lancaster Canal from Town End Bridge.

main street north out of the village to be ditched, drained and generally kept in good repair. By 1785 regular stagecoach services ran through the village from Lancaster to Kendal, Carlisle and Scotland; the Manchester to Carlisle mail coach also passed through Bolton. Despite these better roads and services, many people were dissuaded from using this route by the cost of the tolls, preferring instead to take their chances crossing the sands, a route which remained popular until the mid 19th century and the coming of the railways.

Towards the end of the 18th century a new form of transport, the canal, had a much greater impact on the village. Canal fever had gripped England and in 1792 a bill was passed in Parliament to allow a canal to be built from Kendal to West Houghton, linking the coal of South Lancashire with the limestone of

-LE-SANDS

North Lancashire and Cumbria and enlarging the hinterland of the port of Lancaster. By 1797 Bolton village was on the canal system but at a cost. To avoid the necessity of locks between Preston and Tewitfield and maintain a constant level, the navvies took the canal right through the main road of the village, cutting off Town End. The turnpike was re-routed and new bridges built, giving Main Road through the centre of the village much of its present day structure. At about the same time, the line of the road north of the village was altered, abandoning the steep climb over Thwaite Brow to take the low-level route of the present A6 alongside the canal.

At the time of the first official National Census, in 1801, the population of the village was recorded as 639, most of whom still made their living by farming and/or fishing. Other occupations in the village during the early 19th century served largely local needs or those of travellers by road or canal. Regular passenger transport on the canal, by packet boat, was established in 1820. The desire for faster travel encouraged the packets of the 1830s to reach speeds of 10 mph, necessitating frequent changes of horses giving rise to increased stabling facilities in the village and permanent gangs of labourers to keep the canal banks repaired. Malt kilns processed local barley for the brewing trade and tanneries treated leather, supplying a surprisingly large number (nine) of cordwainers or shoemakers, according to the 1841 National Census. Cinder ovens operated near to the canal and there were still flax-spinners and, of course, a village smithy. The mill near the shore was kept busy and its water power was supplemented at this time by an adjacent windmill.

After over three centuries, the parish church tower was still well preserved but by 1812 the rest of the church was in such disrepair that major rebuilding had to take place and the vast bulk of the present-day church dates from this time; remodelling of the interior and some further extensions took place in 1880. Changes were also taking place in education. The Grammar School building had a general overhaul and the addition of a porch in 1827. Its original strictly classical education was gradually broadened throughout the 1800s to that of a village school catering for the needs of all the boys in the locality – even briefly extending its facilities to a small number of girls.

Meanwhile, in the 1820s, a curate from the parish church made use of the old vicarage turf-house (redundant as peat had been replaced as a fuel by coal brought to the village by canal) to hold a school. He taught reading, writing and arithmetic, providing basic skills for most children and a preparation for the Grammar School for a few. Something similar persisted, educating infants of both sexes and older girls, until 1849 when part of the vicarage land including the turf-house was donated for a new school linked with the church. This became the New Industrial or Crosshill School and consisted of two classrooms, the larger for about seventy girls and the smaller for thirty to forty infants. Although the creation of this school led to improvements in reading and writing, adult literacy remained problematic until the end of the century.

The mid 19th century brought yet another change to the transport system. Although the railway from the south reached Lancaster in 1840, there was a considerable delay while decisions were made about which route to follow north. Proposals included a barrage from Poulton (Morecambe) to Humphrey Head carrying both road and rail. This would have been a major change for the village, cutting it off from the sea and, had it happened, we could now be living on the shores of a lake or looking out over vast flat fields similar to the Dutch polders. However, the route chosen was that we know today, through Carnforth and over Shap to Penrith and Carlisle. Once the decision was made in 1844, five thousand men set to work almost immediately and, amazingly, given difficulties such as crossing the wet, peaty land between village and shore, the line was completed in 1846.

The railway and station were far enough from the main village to leave most roads and buildings untouched, apart from minor changes to Shore and Pasture Lanes and the loss of the old track from St Nicholas Lane to Crag Bank. Despite the distance between village centre and station (situated where the line crosses St Michael's Lane) and the infrequency of stopping trains at first, the railway opened the way for much easier and wider travel; on arriving at Lancaster it was possible to reach most of the country by rail. This very quickly brought about the demise of the packet boat passenger services on the canal. By the 1880s the railway company owned the canal and had also taken over the carriage of most goods; only slow barges with heavy non-perishable loads continued to ply the waterway.

Fishing in the village, especially the collection of cockles, was given a major boost as rail transport allowed the markets of industrial Lancashire and Yorkshire to be reached quickly, giving rise to Bolton's nickname of Cockletown. Education was often neglected in cockling families as even very small children were put to work in these boom years. For many villagers, fishing was often additional to another job so it is impossible to say exactly how many were involved, but the censuses of the time do indicate the changes – in 1841 seven fishermen were recorded but in

1861 the number had risen to forty five. In their search for flat fish, shrimps and cockles the Bolton fishing families often worked alongside similar families around the Bay, leading to considerable intermarriage among the communities.

Cockling in Morecambe Bay.

Before 1840 there was a limited postal service, the mail being carried on foot to and from Lancaster three times a week. With the introduction of Rowland Hill's penny post, paid in advance, a daily service was introduced and a post office established in a cottage at Crosshill. It later moved to a building on Main Road and to its present location in 1940.

The mid 19th century saw attempts to provide villagers with alternatives to the inns and beerhouses for relaxation. A Parochial Temperance Society arranged activities for those signing the pledge; a reading room opened in the evenings at the Grammar School, music classes were held at Crosshill and tuition was also available in reading, writing and accounts. Towards the end of the century a house by Crosshill School was converted to a Reading Room which was available to all men over the age of sixteen at a cost of 2d (<1p) a week or 2s (10p) a quarter. No reading matter could be taken out and no smoking, swearing or gambling was allowed, although some rules were later relaxed. In 1937, the building was demolished for a much-needed extension to the school.

In 1846 the old custom of maypole dancing on the village green had been revived to precede the village sports but this may have been short-lived as, in the latter part of the century and indeed up until the 1930s, the sports were held on Easter Monday and included pace-egg rolling as well as the usual feats of athletic prowess. At other times the churches held concerts and parochial teas followed by entertainments and dancing; there are even records of balls being held at the Blue Anchor.

After the split of the English Church from Rome in the 16th century it had been difficult for people to acknowledge being Roman Catholic. As persecution came to an end during the 18th century, numbers grew steadily until, by the mid 19th

This rather special Sports Day promised a great deal of fun for competitor and spectator alike, with such odd events as Treacle Bun and Cockle races and having to grapple with both greasy poles and a greasy pig's tail. The rewards for success seem quite generous when an agricultural labourer's wage of the time would have been less than £1 a week.

Celebration of the Coronation

Of His Most Gracious Majesty King Edward the VII Emperor of India, and Her Most Gracious Majesty Queen Alexandra.

Township of BOLTON=LE=SANDS.

PROGRAMME OF SPORTS

To be held in connection with the above Celebration in Mr. FISHER'S Field, near the Packet Bridge, Bolton-le-Sands,

On SATURDAY, JUNE 28th, 1902.

TO COMMENCE AT 3 P.M.

...EVENTS...

1.—**100 yards Flat Race Handicap** (trial heats)
Prizes in value, 1st 9s., 2nd 5s., 3rd 2s.

2.—**Long Jump**
Prizes in value, 1st 6s., 2nd 4s., 3rd 2s.

3.—**440 yards Flat Race, Handicap** (trial heats)
Prizes in value, 1st 12s., 2nd 8s., 3rd 5s.

4.—**Age Race, 50 yards Flat Race, Handicap,**
For Men of 60 years of age and over.   Prizes in value 1st 10s., 2nd 6s., 3rd 4s.

5.—**220 yards Flat, Race, Handicap,** for Boys under 16 (trial heats) 5 yards start for each year under 15.   Prizes in value 1st 8s., 2nd 4s., 3rd 2s.

6.—**100 yards Race**   (Final Heat)

7.—**Quoiting Handicap,** distance 18 yards, Handicapper : Mr. A. Long.   Prizes in value, 1st 10s,, 2nd 6s., 3rd 4s.

8.—**Six a side Football Contest** 10 minutes each way. (Association Rules) to be competed for in skirts.   Prizes in value 1st 12s.. 2nd 6s.

9.—**Treacle Bun Race.**
Prizes in value 1st 6s., 2nd 4s., 3rd 2s.

10.—**440 yards Flat Race** (Final Heat).

11.—**220 yards Flat Race, Handicap,** for Boys under 16 (Final Heat)

12.—**Cockle Race,**
Prizes in value. 1st 6s., 2nd 4s., 3rd 2s.

13.—**100 yards Flat Race, Handicap,** for Boys under 12 years of age.   Prizes in value, 1st 5s., 2nd 3s., 3rd 2s., 4th 1s.

14.—**100 yards Flat Race, Handicap,** for Girls from 12 to 15 years of age,   Prizes in value 1st 6s., 2nd 4s., 3rd 2s., 4th 1s,

15.—**75 yards Flat Race, Handicap,** for Girls from 8 to 12 years of age.   Prizes in value, 1st 5s.. 2nd 3/6, 3rd 2/6, 4th 1/6, 5th 1s.

16.—**Sack Race,**
Prizes in value, 1st 7s., 2nd 5s., 3rd 3s.

17.—**Women's Egg and Spoon Race,** 50 yards, Prizes in value, 1st 6s., 2nd 4s., 3rd 2s.

18.—**Three-Legged Race,** 200 yards, Handicap, Prizes in value, 1st 9s., 2nd 6s., 3rd 4s.

19.—**Throwing the Cricket Ball,**
Prizes in value, 1st 5s., 2nd 3s., 3rd 2s.

20.—**Obstacle Race,**
Prizes in value, 1st 7/6, 2nd 5/-, 3rd 2/6.

21.—**Climbing Greasy Pole,**
Prizes to the value, of 10s.

22.—**Catching Pig with greasy tail,**
Prize in value, 1st 7/6.

23.—**Consolation Race,** Handicap open to Non-winners 300 yards. Prizes in value, 1st 7/6, 2nd 5/-, 3rd 2/6.

24.—**Fancy Dress Cycle Parade,**
Prizes in value, 1st 18/-, 2nd 12/-, 3rd 6/-, 4th 4s. To start from Cross Hill at 8-45 p.m.

Maypole Dances at intervals.

All Competitors to have been bona fide residents of the Township of Bolton-le-Sands, for Three Months previous to the 28th June, 1902.

Entry Fee for each competitor over 12 years of age to be **3d.** each, which will be returned when ready to compete.

All competitors 12 years of age and under, FREE.   Entries under 12 years of age to be made on the field.

Last Day for Entries, over 12 years of age, Saturday, June 21st, 1902.

century there were sufficient to want their own church in the village rather than travel to Lancaster or Yealand Conyers. For sixteen years from 1868, a barn in the Nook was used for worship until a site became available at Crosshill. The land and buildings of an old property known as Statters were cleared and the church of St Mary of the Angels, described as 'one of the most beautiful village churches in England' was completed in 1884. In 1895 a small school opened on Kellet Lane for thirty three Roman Catholic children who had previously had to attend the Grammar School or Crosshill School, both with strong Anglican connections.

In the second half of the 19th century there were also two schools for young ladies, most of whom were boarders. One, running for about twenty years from the mid 1870s, was at The Cottage by the canal; the other ran from the mid 1860s at Red Bank House until it was taken over by the Church of England Waifs and Strays Society in 1899 and opened as a home for young girls which survived until just after World War I.

A large piece of common land of about two hectares on Thwaite Brow had always been used by the villagers for their cattle which, by the 19th century, had led to serious overgrazing. In 1829, to resolve the problem, it was decided to let the grazing rights by auction and use the money generated for the benefit of the village. A fund was set up to pay for inquests and funerals for bodies washed up on the shore – as well as to employ a village mole-catcher. Many villagers were reluctant to give up their rights and continued, if not to graze cattle, then to dig for the gravel found just below the turf. At the end of the century the newly established Parish Council took control of the land and let it as a poultry run.

It is at some time during the 19th century that *Bolton-le-Sands* finally came into being. The Anglo-Saxon *Bodeltone* had become *Boulton* or *Bolton* but this name was shared with numerous other settlements in the North West alone. Attempts by church and legal authorities in the Middle Ages to make some distinction led to additions such as *in Lonsdale*, *by the Sandes* or *neere the Sandes*; if the classical scholars of the day had had their way we could have been living in *Bolton super Arenas* or *Bolton-in-Sabulis*. By the early 19th century the names used had been reduced to three: *Bolton*, *Bolton by the Sands* and *Bolton-le-Sands* and, by the end of the century, the last had been universally accepted.

At this point, before considering the major changes which have taken place in the 20th and 21st centuries, it may be interesting to look at a snap shot of village life revealed by the 1901 National Census – a time which coincides roughly with the birth of the picture postcard, one of the main sources of illustration for this book.

Bolton-le-Sands just before the 1901 National Census
(adapted from the 1895 Ordnance Survey Map)

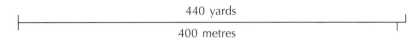

440 yards

400 metres

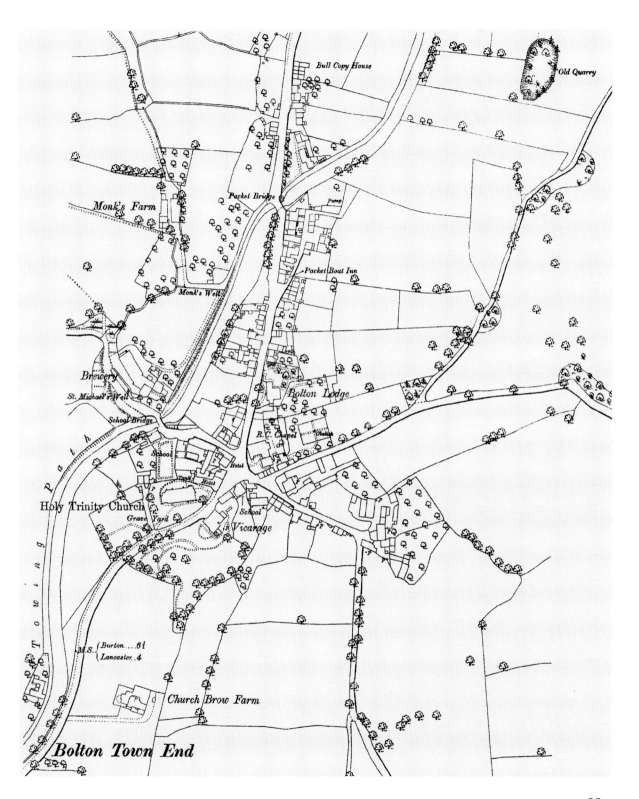

Bull Copy House

Old Quarry

Monk's Farm

Packet Bridge

Pump

Packet Boat Inn

Monk's Well

Brewery

St. Michael's Well

Bolton Lodge

School Bridge

R.C. Chapel

Obelisk

School

Hotel

Hotel

Holy Trinity Church

Grave Yard

School

Vicarage

Towing Path

M.S. { Burton...6¼
Lancaster..4

Church Brow Farm

Bolton Town End

23

The population consisted of just over nine hundred persons with slightly more females than males, the numbers of young females perhaps being swollen by the inhabitants of the Victoria Home for Waifs and Strays and those in service or looking after elderly relatives. Over 9% of villagers had reached at least 60 years of age and a stalwart five had reached their eighties, the eldest being 87. This is negligible compared with today's population but does indicate an ongoing improvement in living conditions as the elderly component of the village was about one and a half times that of fifty years earlier. At the same time the proportion of young people was falling from around half being under 20 in 1851 to just over 40% in 1901.

Age structure in 1901

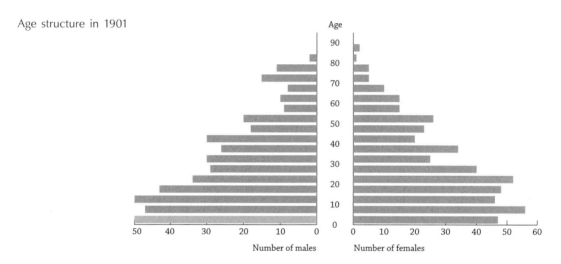

Number of males   Number of females

Some comparisons between 1901 and 2001

	1901	2001
Total population	902	4159
Number of households	206	1783
Mean number per household	4·38	2·33
% children and teenagers	42·90	21·67
% aged 65–84	6·32	17·58
% aged 85+	0·22	2·16

Family size had tended to shrink from the large numbers of the early 19th century and the most common household size was two persons, although five or six children per family was not uncommon and one fishing family could boast nine offspring between the ages of 5 and 19. Many households included extended family of at least three generations living together, often with additional in-laws and nephews and nieces. About a quarter of households had servants living on the premises; many of the better off had several – the vicarage employed a cook, kitchenmaid, housemaid, parlourmaid and page. Some families took in, as boarders, people working in the locality such as a painter and decorator, originally from London, lodging with a young couple in Town End, or a local carter without his own home lodging with a fishing family on Main Road.

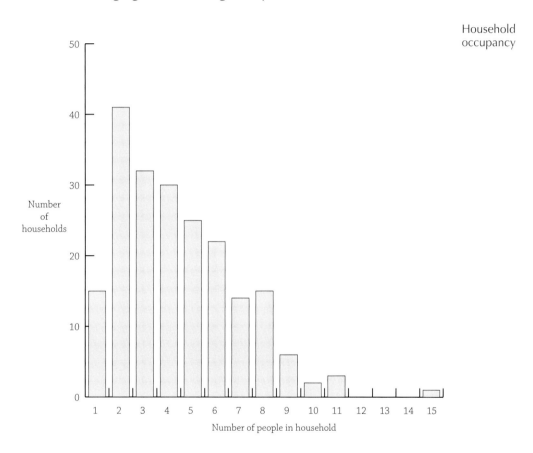

Household occupancy

About 40% of the villagers could claim Bolton-le-Sands as their birthplace, more than half of these being of school age or younger. We tend to imagine that prior to the 20th century village populations were not very mobile and people did not venture far from home. A glance at the places of origin of the 1901 Boltoners would indicate the lack of truth in this; in only five married couples were both partners born in Bolton-le-Sands. Although marriage patterns revealed strong links with other local villages and towns such as Nether Kellet, Carnforth and Lancaster and with other fishing communities, particularly Flookburgh, a substantial minority of inhabitants came from much further afield: the policeman and his wife hailed from Scotland, the vicar came from London and his wife from New Zealand, servants from Cornwall and Ireland, bank clerks from Sunderland, farm labourers from Manchester and fishermen from Liverpool.

Birthplace of Bolton-le-Sands residents in 1901

Place of Birth	%	Cumulative %
Bolton-le-Sands	40·5	40·5
Within 5 miles of Bolton-le-Sands	18·5	59·0
5 -10 miles from Bolton-le-Sands	8·4	67·4
10 – 20 miles from Bolton-le-Sands	9·8	77·2
20 – 50 miles from Bolton-le-Sands	8·8	86·0
Elsewhere in Great Britain	12·0	98·0
Ireland	1·3	99·3
Elsewhere in the World	0·7	100

Around two fifths of the population were indicated as working. A sizeable minority (4.4%) classed themselves as retired or living on their own means. The rest naturally included children although when childhood ended is unclear. At the age of 13 several had already found employment as servants, messengers or farm workers and it was deemed necessary to indicate on the census that they were single; other 13 year olds could still be in education or, in the case of girls, be at home helping run the household. At certain times of year even younger children would be removed from school to help with fishing and farming activities. Many women appeared among the non-employed because domestic work within one's own home, however difficult, was not recorded.

Of the occupations listed, domestic service took the largest share; some workers had very specific titles such as nursery governess or cook but more often they were simply classed as general servants. Agriculture and fishing continued to be important and, along with construction and repair of buildings, occupied large numbers of men. The shops and other local services such as the post office and inns provided jobs for both men and women while the local railway and Carnforth Iron Works were also significant employers. Among the more unusual occupations listed for villagers were landscape painter, assistant anylist (sic), spice merchant and meat trade outfitter/agent for thermal baths and cattle foods.

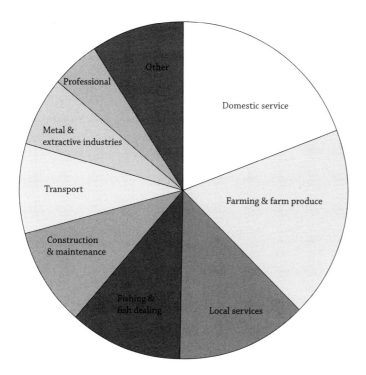

This picture started to change, slowly at first up until World War I and very much more rapidly after World War II. As education took on a greater importance fewer children neglected their studies to pick cockles and potatoes and started to seek employment outside fishing and farming. Girls began to find jobs in shops and offices rather than domestic service. Motor transport, in the shape of a bus service (begun in 1922) passing through the centre of the village, enabled people to travel easily, directly and frequently to Lancaster without having to walk across the fields to the railway station and this started the trend towards Bolton-le-Sands becoming a commuter village instead of the tightly-knit, self-sufficient community of previous generations.

By the second decade of the 20th century the railway was providing a relatively cheap and more frequent service than in its early days and continued to provide competition for road transport, especially for longer journeys. Holiday makers arrived in large numbers by train; between the World Wars, during Wakes weeks in industrial Lancashire and Yorkshire, every available bed in the village could be taken, with camping sites springing up by the shore or in friendly farmers' fields. After the 1950s motor transport increased dramatically and rail was used far less; in 1969 Bolton-le-Sands station closed and today there is hardly any sign of its existence.

At the beginning of the 20th century the roads through the village were simply made of material supplied by farmers ridding their fields of stone which was then steamrollered flat. When vehicles with rubber tyres drove along these roads, especially in dry weather, they created a great deal of dust so, in 1911, the Parish Council sprayed the roads with tar and brought in a 10 mph speed limit. The general increase in traffic and the mingling of motorcars, buses and lorries with horse-drawn carts, pedestrians and bicycles brought congestion to Main Road as, at this time, it was still the main north–south route. Packet Bridge became a serious bottleneck and a string of accidents led to a suggestion of widening the road in 1919. Difficulties with property owners along the route prevented this and the plan was abandoned in favour of a bypass. Lack of funds delayed the beginning of work until 1926 and the new road was eventually completed in September 1928. At its opening it was stated that road traffic in Bolton-le-Sands had doubled since 1924 and risen sixteen-fold since 1917.

Bolton-le-Sands railway station in the early 20th century, complete with signal box, footbridge and employees.

Bolton-le-Sands Station.

The education of the village children in the early 20th century continued to be divided between the three principal village schools. The Grammar School was equipped with lighting, water and heating and despite the cramped conditions and the desire of the Local Education Authority to close it, the school survived through the 1920s and 1930s. After legislation in 1936 removed the boys over the age of 11, numbers became too low to be viable and the decision was made to use funds from the Grammar School Trustees to enlarge Crosshill School to take junior boys as well as girls. Crosshill School had fared rather better for facilities as, by the late 1930s, it had both central heating and electric lighting. The extensions to accommodate the boys were finished in 1939 but the war intervened and their places were occupied by evacuees from Salford. The Grammar School finally closed and the boys moved to Crosshill, renamed Bolton-le-Sands Church of England Mixed School, in autumn 1940.

The Roman Catholic School experienced steady growth throughout the 1920s and 1930s, many children coming by bus from outside the village, and was therefore forced to expand into other nearby buildings. It too welcomed evacuees at the beginning of World War II.

The 20th century brought changes in the former mainstays of employment, fishing and farming. Overfishing had resulted in declining catches so that people had to travel further out into the bay and for longer to try and make a living. As time went by, attempts were made to improve efficiency in reaching the fishing grounds by using tractors and jeeps instead of horses and carts. Ex-military, amphibious, tracked vehicles were tried but with little success and as supplies of these and their spare parts dried up so did the fishing and people turned to less hazardous and uncertain occupations.

With competition from cheap imported foreign grain, cereal growing had been largely replaced by livestock. Despite brief revivals of arable farming in the drive for self-sufficiency during the two World Wars, this has remained the picture to the present day. With increased mechanisation, fewer labourers were required on the land and employment in the agricultural sector shrank rapidly.

The 20th century saw the building of the third of Bolton-le-Sands main churches. Nonconformists had officially been tolerated since the 17th century but were often viewed with suspicion by the establishment. Various houses were registered as meeting places but nothing permanent was established. Towards the end of the 19th century, the pastor of Carnforth Congregational Church rented Laurel House in Bolton-le-Sands and started a mission in the loft of his stable there. Some years later, on his retirement, the same pastor returned to live in the village and became determined to build a Free Church here. A corrugated iron building was bought from Morecambe fairground and erected on land made available behind St Michael's Grove, becoming known as the Tin Tabernacle. Inspired by a bequest in a will, further fundraising enabled a new site on Main Road to be purchased and a new permanent building, Christ Church, was finally opened in 1935.

There had been steady growth in the population of Bolton-le-Sands, reaching around 1150 in 1931 but, more noticeably, the village itself was starting to grow. Despite shrinking family size, many people were no longer content to live in small cottages and semi-detached housing began to appear on greenfield sites, especially alongside the major roads leading out of the village. The main growth spurt, however, came after World War II and whole farms disappeared, their land swallowed up beneath housing estates such as the Church Brow estate to the south of the village; after the closure of the watermill in the late 1960s and the draining of the long-redundant Mill Dam, huge numbers of houses were built on the western side.

Housing built on the western side of the bypass in the 1960s

ST. MICHAELS ESTATE. BOLTON-LE-SANDS.

The influx of new families placed extra demands on services such as education. Both schools had seen their numbers rise and neither school had room to expand. The Catholic school abandoned its scattered buildings and the children transferred to a new school in Carnforth. For the Church of England school additional classrooms were built on Mount Pleasant Lane in 1967 with more rooms added in the 1970s as numbers continued to grow. Eventually the Mount Pleasant Lane site was able to accommodate all the children on roll and the old school at Crosshill was closed, to be converted to housing in 1995.

Despite electricity reaching Bolton-le-Sands in 1930, there was no street lighting until 1961. A purpose-built library arrived in 1973 and a new doctors' surgery at Brookfield ten years later. Both the police and the fire service moved out of the village centre to the southern outskirts and the bypass road respectively. The extension of the M6 motorway north of Lancaster helped remove some of the north-south traffic from the A6 passing through the village.

In 1944 a committee was formed to raise money to provide a village amenity to welcome those soon to return home from the forces at the end of World War II. The bulk of the money was used to buy the land which makes up the village playing fields, whose ownership was transferred to the Parish Council in 1948. A children's playground was built to replace the one on Main Road: football and, briefly, cricket pitches were levelled (the cricket club moved to their own ground off Main Road in 1953): tennis courts were laid and finally, in 1981, a bowling green appeared. One of the most important village institutions, the Community Centre, was opened next to the playing fields in 1976.

Another area of the village associated with leisure is Thwaite Brow. In the early 20th century its park-like appearance was enjoyed by villagers and holidaymakers alike but during World War II it became overgrown. By the 1980s, the viewpoints were choked with vegetation, the seats were lost and the paths were in disrepair. Now, with the aid of volunteers, it has become a public amenity once again. The canal too has become a leisure facility; no goods traffic has passed through Bolton-le-Sands since World War II (the last coal barges arriving in Lancaster in 1947) and so the waterway has been used by pleasure craft and its banks by fishermen, walkers and cyclists. Since the extension of the M6 north of Carnforth the northern reaches of the canal have been cut off and boats can proceed no further than Tewitfield. In 2002 a link was opened allowing boats to cross the Ribble Estuary without being lifted from the water, thus connecting the Lancaster Canal with the rest of the English canal network. There are ambitious

Population growth

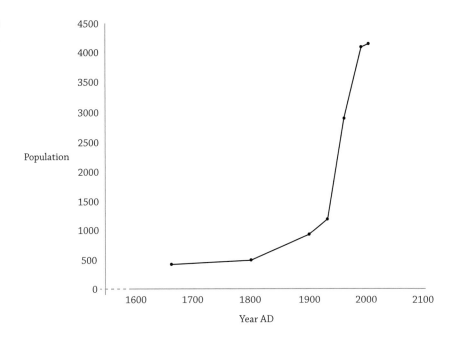

plans to re-open the northern stretch of the canal for boats once again to reach Kendal, but this will be a long and costly operation so it will be many years before any discernible change is seen in canal traffic. Briefly, in the early years of the 21st century, a waterbus plied a regular service between Carnforth and Lancaster passing through Bolton-le-Sands.

The changes initiated at the beginning of the 20th century have shaped today's 21st century village. The population now stands at a little over 4000 and the original village centre has been dwarfed by the expansion of the built-up area. Few inhabitants make their living in the village itself; most workers commute to Lancaster or Kendal or further afield via the motorway or by rail, many in occupations completely unknown in 1901. There are still farms but their labour requirements are low and not all farmers' incomes derive strictly from their husbandry; farm shops and cafés have appeared in redundant barns, while numerous fields support caravans instead of crops. In some cases, especially after the foot-and-mouth epidemic of 2001 and the alteration of subsidies for land, cows and sheep have been replaced by small stables of horses or ponies. The role of the garden centre has grown at the expense of market gardening.

Although some villagers still collect shrimps on a small scale, fishing is mainly a recreational pastime with rod and line along the canal or in the specially created anglers' pond. Periodically the cockle beds offshore at Bolton-le-Sands are opened but the tragedy of the Chinese cockle-pickers drowned in 2004 illustrates the fact that it was not village fishermen but strangers with no knowledge of the difficult conditions in the bay who were sent out to gather shellfish, not for the local or even the British market but for export to Spain.

The M6 has long replaced the A6 as the main north-south route but traffic has continued to increase. The number of parked cars in the narrow main street causes problems for both pedestrians and large vehicles; most service buses no longer pass through the village centre and are restricted to the bypass. A set of traffic lights has replaced the early 20th-century policeman at Packet Bridge.

Despite the changes, Bolton-le-Sands remains a village, albeit a relatively large one. It continues to support a variety of shops and services including a post office, churches, public houses, restaurants and cafés. The old village smithy still exists alongside more modern machinery and is occasionally used to produce specialised items. Village children are still able to attend a village school. The Community Centre, church halls and the old Grammar School (now converted into a small meeting centre) are well used by local societies and the village is represented in a number of sporting leagues. Although the community no longer comes together for an annual sports' day and maypole dancing, events such as the Summer Gala and the Bonfire and Fireworks in November still draw in the crowds.

Unfortunately the demands of 21st-century living can bring conflict. The pressing need to find employment leads to commuting further afield and the use of services nearer to work, with the consequent decline in the fortunes of providers in the village. The cost of property locally and elsewhere in the region has made it difficult for young people to afford homes here and there is a constant demand for more housing with developers anxious to nibble at the edges of the built-up area. It would be a great pity if this century should see the end of a village, which has certainly existed for more than ten centuries, as it becomes swallowed up into the suburbs of Greater Lancaster as has already happened with the old villages of Skerton and Scotforth.

Address.

The Village in Pictures

These few introductory pictures give a general overview of Bolton-le-Sands in its setting. The sections which follow look in more detail at different aspects of village life.

The photographer has climbed to the top of the tower of Holy Trinity Church to take this view of the village looking north, reproduced on a card sent to Ormskirk in 1905. Sheep graze peacefully in the field now occupied by Bolton-le-Sands library.

Bolton-le-Sands.

Another view from Holy Trinity's tower, posted to Rampside, near Barrow, in 1914. In this wintry scene a light coating of snow lingers on the roofs of the houses and dusts the fields beyond the Church of St Mary of the Angels.

Pictured from a hill behind The Nook, the spire of St Mary's of the Angels rises above the rooftops of the village on a 1908 card sent to Newcastle. Crosshill School, the old parish hall and houses in The Nook are the nearest buildings, while Warton Crag can be seen in the distance.

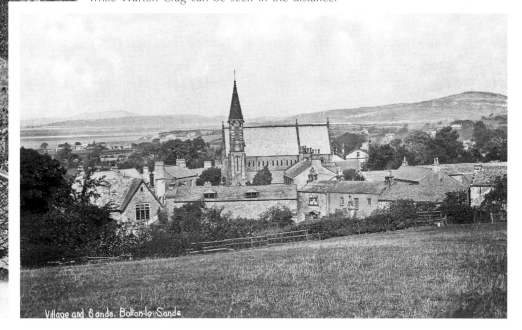

Distant View, Bolton-le-Sands.

In this 'Distant View' of the village taken in 1925, the buildings on Packet Hill are just visible across the fields from the Mill Dam, a meeting place of three streams which fed the watermill near the shore.

The northern end of Bolton-le-Sands between Bridge House on Packet Hill and Thwaite Brow viewed from above Monkswell Farm around 1930. The field in the centre of the picture is now the village cricket ground while the foreground is occupied by houses at the top of St Michael's Close.

BOLTON-LE-SANDS.

The wooded slopes of Thwaite Brow seen from Main Road near Whin Grove around 1925 – a view that today would be partially obscured by the houses of Eden Grove. Until the early years of the 20th century Thwaite Brow, the largest area of common land in the parish, would have been virtually treeless. This was due partly to cattle owners exercising their right to graze animals without any control on numbers and partly to the removal of turf by villagers to gain access to the underlying gravel deposits (the scar of a once extensive gravel quarry is discernible below the telegraph poles in the photograph).

View from the Brow, Bolton-le-Sands.

A double-decker bus on its way to the village passes below Thwaite Brow. Its elevated location made the Brow a popular recreational spot for village residents and holiday makers who walked its paths and enjoyed the panoramic views over Morecambe Bay. Looking west towards Furness only the occasional cottage interrupts a landscape dominated by fields and hedges, a landscape that would be totally transformed by the housing estates of the 1960s and 1970s.

Town End contains several attractive old cottages, a number of which are Grade II listed. Once on the main road through Bolton-le-Sands it was severed from the rest of the village by the building of the Lancaster Canal in 1797 and today is a quiet cul-de-sac.

Red Bank shore and the 'Elephant Rock' photographed in the 1920s. The extent of the salt marsh has continually fluctuated as it responds to the changing channels in Morecambe Bay. Today it has virtually disappeared from below Red Bank which itself is slowly receding as rain washes out the stones from the exposed cliff face.

THE SHORE, BOLTON LE SANDS.

In this rather desolate scene low tide has exposed the mud flats and meandering channels at the edge of the salt marsh near Red Bank Farm. The copse of bare trees would afford the farm buildings some protection from the cold northerly winds in winter.

Fishing and Farming

Robert 'Catty Bob' Wilson and his wife Lizzie set out across the salt marsh from their cottage on Thwaite Brow. Cockles were much in demand from the industrial towns of Lancashire and the West Riding and consignments left every day from local stations. However, the cockle beds can vary in location and quality and are particularly susceptible to overfishing, factors which caused the near collapse of the fishery between the wars. Catches of flat fish also declined at this time for the same reason and the number of local people working the sands shrank as it became increasingly difficult to achieve a reasonable standard of living.

BOLTON SHORE.

A solitary horse-drawn cart makes its way to the shore near Red Bank, returning from a day's fishing out in the bay. When this card was posted in 1910 more than a score of local families were making a living fishing in the shallow waters for plaice, flukes and shrimps, or collecting cockles from the mud once the tide had ebbed. Some of the catch was sold in the village but the majority went either to Lancaster or was sent by rail to Preston and further afield.

Tommy, the Wilson's horse, waits patiently as his owners gather cockles. Cockling involved the use of a number of specialised implements. A wooden board with handles, called a jumbo, was rocked to and fro on the wet sand to bring the cockles to the surface. They were then scooped into a basket or tiernel by means of a curved, three-pronged fork known as a craam.

Another well-known family 'living from the sands' were the Burrows of Smithy House. In this photograph from 1948 Robert Burrow, nicknamed 'Cockle Bob', watches a catch being riddled to return the immature individuals to the sea. In the background is an ex-Army amphibious tracked vehicle called a Weasel which Robert bought to cut the time taken to reach the fishing grounds. Capable of more than 30 mph over difficult terrain it was ideal for the sands of Morecambe Bay but was also susceptible to breakdowns caused by salt water corrosion.

Tel. 236 Hest Bank.

R. BURROW,
FISH AND FRUIT DEALER.

SMITHY HOUSE,
BOLTON - LE - SANDS,
Nr, LANCASTER.

Liz Burrow and her dog Tony outside Smithy House in 1956. Known as 'Mrs Cockle Bob' she often went out on the sands with her husband until starting a family. Of her four children the youngest, Dick Burrow, was the last fisherman based in the village, using a tractor to trawl for shrimps and stake nets to catch flatfish. He had a fish and greengrocery business to market his catch and also hawked his fish around Lancaster.

Although this card is titled Coxes Farm, the name is slightly inaccurate, being a misspelling of Cock's Farm. The Cock family had been at what is now called Red Bank Farm since the mid 19th century and in 1910, when this card was posted, it was being run by brothers William and John Cock who had taken over the farm from their parents John and Elizabeth.

William Cock poses with one of his prize sheep at Red Bank Farm. While lambing was done close to the farmhouse, for most of the year the adult sheep were allowed to wander freely on the salt marsh where local farmers had grazing rights. By the beginning of the 20th century sheep and dairy cattle had largely replaced cereal crops as the mainstay of agriculture in the parish.

This view of Red Bank Farm from the shore is much the same now as it was when this card was sent nearly a century ago. The farmhouse dates from 1680 and is thought to be one of two originally on the site, the other being the birthplace of local diarist William Stout. Since the end of World War II, Red Bank Farm has been owned by the Archer family. In recent years declining farm incomes have seen the Archers diversify and farming activities are now supplemented by a caravan site and a popular café and shop.

A little further along the coast, where Mill Lane curves round to meet St Nicholas Lane, is a farm which has undergone several name changes during its existence. On this card and on the 1930 Ordnance Survey map it is The Grange. In Victorian times it was known as Mill Stile House before being listed as Beach House in the 1901 Census. Today it is called Wild Duck Hall, no longer a working farm but an equestrian centre which offers horse-riding lessons and other equine facilities. Tom was staying with relatives at The Grange when he wrote home to Lytham in April 1920: *'I am having a lovely time. Uncle let the pigs out this morning and they did romp about. Lady the cat is blind now but the dog Nipper and I are quite friendly.'*

The Grange.
Bolton-le-Sands.

Haymaking was usually carried out in June and July. Once cut and dried the hay was loaded onto a cart and taken back to the farm. It was a busy time, with friends and older children all helping with the work. Here three generations of the same family are photographed in 1920 in a hayfield belonging to farmer Thomas Whiteside of Mossdale. He is standing on the extreme left next to his son William while his young grandson Walter looks down from the top of the hay cart.

Two year old Walter Whiteside also appears in this picture. He is with Jack Taylor and Nelly the horse as they cut the grass in Doctor's Meadow, a large field which today is covered by the houses and gardens of Whin Avenue. Springwell Cottage can be seen in the background.

Steel ploughshares were introduced in the mid 19th century enabling deeper and wider furrows to be turned to produce more soil so that better crops could be grown. It was during this period that ploughing competitions were born. They were mostly parish affairs with prizes awarded to the ploughmen who could cut the straightest and most consistent furrows. Ploughing matches became important events in the agricultural calendar and drew many spectators, including children who were often allowed out of school to attend.

Prize Ploughing Bolton-le-Sands 1905

A number of farmhouses were located in the village itself with their fields stretching some distance away. One such was Coupland's farm in Town End. The house itself dates from 1640 and is now Grade II listed. After World War II it was sold and became the Old Farm Guest House which offered accommodation to holidaymakers until the mid 1970s.

Pictured outside the farmhouse in about 1905 is farmer Thomas Coupland, his wife Ann and daughters Mary Jane and Isabella.

THE MILL, BOLTON-LE-SANDS

Most local farmers used the watermill at the seaward end of Mill Lane to process their grain. While a watermill has probably stood on the site since the Middle Ages, the present building dates from the early years of the 19th century when it was advertised for lease as 'a newly erected watermill, the machinery newly constructed and comprising two pairs of grit stones and one pair of French stones, the flour cylinder, also a drying kiln.' The different types of grinding stones indicate that the mill was capable of producing both oatmeal and wheat flour. By the 1880s the waterwheel was being assisted by a steam engine for which a tall brick chimney had been erected in the adjacent field. Richard Ayrton was miller and corn merchant at this time, remaining in charge until well into his seventies. The mill continued to be run by members of the Ayrton family, using a variety of power sources, until its eventual closure in 1967. Today nothing remains of the mill machinery and the building is now used as a furniture store.

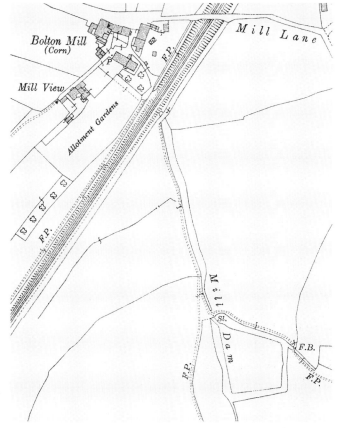

The watermill was fed by three streams which flowed into a pond known as the Mill Dam at the end of which a sluice gate controlled the amount of water reaching the waterwheel.

The stile marks the line of a footpath which ran from Main Road to the shore, close to the mill chimney in the distance. When the mill ceased working, the Mill Dam was filled in and the streams piped underground, to be covered in the 1970s by the bungalows and semi-detached houses of Lowlands Road, Shelley Close and the central part of Sunnybank Road.

Cattle graze contentedly in the damp pastures next to the Mill Dam. In the spring the fields would be yellow with celandines and buttercups with marsh marigolds and irises at the water's edge, to be followed by the deeper colours of the clovers and vetches of summer. Reeds would offer hiding places and nesting sites for waterfowl while the pond itself would yield frogspawn and sticklebacks to children with their makeshift fishing nets and string-handled jam jars.

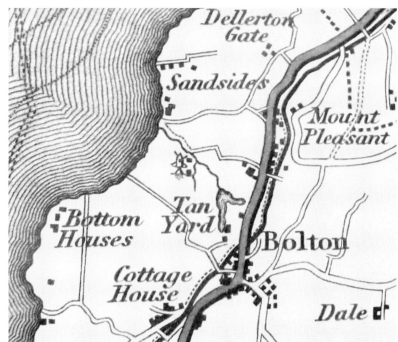

Close to the watermill, on slightly higher ground, was a windmill. It is shown on G. Hennet's 1828 map of Lancashire and made the news in December of that year when the *Lancaster Gazette* reported that during a violent thunderstorm 'lightning struck the windmill at Bolton-by-the-Sands, carrying away the shafts with the sails, etc and doing other considerable damage – the fields, etc were thickly covered with hailstones for sometime afterwards. Fortunately no person was injured.' Repairs were carried out and the windmill worked for a few more years before eventually closing in about 1850. The need for two mills suggests that cereal crops were once grown more widely in the parish, confirmation of which can be found on the Tithe Map of 1846 which shows that over a quarter of the farmland was occupied by oats, barley and wheat.

Bolton-le-Sands

CARD

Address.

Religion

PARISH CHURCH . BOLTON-LE-S

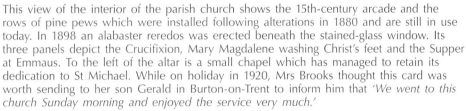

This view of the interior of the parish church shows the 15th-century arcade and the rows of pine pews which were installed following alterations in 1880 and are still in use today. In 1898 an alabaster reredos was erected beneath the stained-glass window. Its three panels depict the Crucifixion, Mary Magdalene washing Christ's feet and the Supper at Emmaus. To the left of the altar is a small chapel which has managed to retain its dedication to St Michael. While on holiday in 1920, Mrs Brooks thought this card was worth sending to her son Gerald in Burton-on-Trent to inform him that *'We went to this church Sunday morning and enjoyed the service very much.'*

One of only two Grade II* listed buildings in the village – the other being Hawkshead Farmhouse – Bolton-le-Sands parish church has a long history. While a church is known to have stood here in Norman times the present building is much more recent. Externally its oldest part is the sandstone tower which dates from the late 15th century (the clock faces were added in 1837). Also surviving from this time are the pillars and arches between the nave and the north aisle in the body of the church, known as the arcade. All the rest is 19th century in origin. In 1812 the building was found to be in such a poor state that virtually everything except the above mentioned had to be replaced. Restoration took four years, from 1813 to 1817. Further structural alterations and additions were carried out over the ensuing decades during which time, for some unexplained reason, the long-standing name of the church underwent a change from St Michael's to Holy Trinity. This card was posted to Formby in 1905 with the disquieting message *'This is the church where poor Isobel and George were married'*. One wonders what befell *'poor Isobel'*!

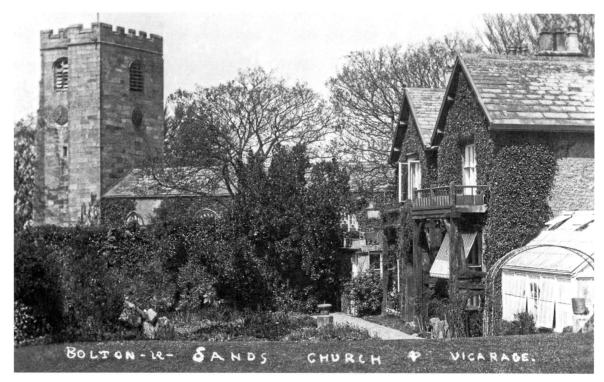

BOLTON-le-SANDS CHURCH & VICARAGE.

Across the road from Holy Trinity Church was the vicarage, a substantial building set in its own spacious grounds. In 1911, the year this card was sent to Leeds, the vicar was the Reverend Arthur Tomlinson who had arrived in Bolton-le-Sands in 1899 with his wife and three children. He had sufficient means to employ five servants to look after the needs of his family, including a page and a kitchenmaid who had accompanied him from his previous post in Cornwall. Built in 1830 the vicarage remained the home of the incumbent until 1949 when the house and grounds were sold, having become unsuitable for modern requirements and very costly to maintain. Alternative accommodation was acquired in Ancliffe Lane and the vicarage was turned into a children's home. However, recent developments have seen the old building completely refurbished and half of it restored to its original use as the vicarage for the parish church.

The Roman Catholic Church of St Mary of the Angels, with its 25-metre spire, dominates the centre of the village. Catholics started meeting in a converted barn at the head of The Nook in 1868 but it soon became apparent that a larger building was required. When a piece of land came up for sale at Crosshill it was purchased by wealthy spinster Miss Anne Coulston of Hawkshead House. She also bore the entire cost of constructing the new church as well as buying an adjoining plot on Kellet Lane for use as a cemetery. Built of Yorkshire freestone in the Gothic Revival style, St Mary's was consecrated by the Bishop of Leeds in 1884 and described in the *Lancaster Guardian* as 'one of the most beautiful ecclesiastical edifices in the diocese'. This card, sent to Bradford in 1921, shows the original entrance gateway to the church.

Roman Catholic Church. Bolton-le-sands. "Key" series.

St. Mary of the Angels Church, Bolton-le-Sands.

The interior of St Mary's is equally impressive. The clerestoried nave consists of five arches resting on massive pillars of polished granite, the base and capitals of which are of dressed York stone. On the arches are carved images of various saints. The highly decorative reredos behind the altar is of alabaster, marble and Bath stone and contains two panels in which are representations of The Assumption and The Coronation of the Virgin Mary.

Designed by local architect H. Wareing Pennington in the plain modernist style of the 1930s, Christ Church Congregational Church was the lasting legacy of Nonconformist pastor William Towers. Since his arrival in Bolton-le-Sands in 1880 he had always wanted a permanent place of worship in the village for Congregationalists. Following a bequest from his brother-in-law and active fund raising on his part (despite being in his late seventies) William Towers acquired enough funds to purchase a site on Main Road overlooking Morecambe Bay. Five years in the construction, Christ Church was officially opened by Mrs Towers in 1935. In 1959 the building was enlarged to improve the amenities of the premises and in 1972 it became the United Reform Church following the amalgamation of the Congregational Church of England and Wales and the Presbyterian Churches of England.

Before the completion of Christ Church in 1935 the Congregationalists of the village met in a corrugated iron building known as the 'Tin Tabernacle'. Bought by William Towers for £40 from Morecambe Fairground, it was re-erected on land next to the canal near Packet Bridge and opened for worship in 1910. The drawing is by J. W. Towers, great-nephew of William Towers.

Christ Church, Congregational, Bolton-le-Sands

CARD

Address.

Education

CANAL
BOLTON LE SANDS

Pictured in 1905 from across the canal, the 'Old Boys School' (on the left) originated from a bequest by Thomas Assheton and was opened in 1637. It was properly titled the Free Grammar School as all boys from the village, Nether Kellet and Slyne-with-Hest were admitted free for education in Latin and Greek. If, however, they wanted instruction in reading, writing or arithmetic a fee had to be paid to the Master. This situation stayed much the same for the next 200 years until the middle of the 19th century when the character of the school began to change to more of a village school with the emphasis on the three 'Rs', although fees were still required. By this time conditions in the building were rather primitive and cramped and, according to the Trustees, 'unfit for the well conducting of the School', a concern which resulted in the construction of a much needed extension in 1857. In 1875 the decision was taken to apply for recognition as a Public Elementary School which entitled the school to financial assistance in the form of a government grant. This allowed fees to be reduced to a modest level and enabled the school to 'provide Books, Copies, Slates, Pens, Ink, etc. and supply them to the children free of charge'. Around the date the postcard was produced there were 43 children on roll and the school was given permission to employ an assistant mistress to help with the teaching.

The iron railings have long gone but the building has hardly changed externally since this photograph was taken in 1925.

61

On 1st September 1937 the Grammar School commemorated its 300th anniversary and silver medals with blue ribbons were presented to the 45 children and two teachers. Celebrations, however, were short-lived. Legislation the previous year foreshadowed the removal of pupils of eleven-plus age from all-age schools and as a result the Grammar School's numbers were considered to be too low for it to continue. In September 1940 the children moved out to join those at Crosshill School.

A small walled patch of ground across the road from the Grammar School (now a parking area) was cultivated by the children as a mixed vegetable and flower garden, although it had become rather neglected and overgrown by the time the school closed. After its discontinuation as a school the building was used as a wartime Home Guard headquarters and later as a branch library. Today, it provides a meeting place for various village organisations, including the Parish Council.

View from School Bridge, Bolton-le-Sands.

Until the passing of the 1870 Education Act which introduced compulsory education for children between five and ten years of age, most teaching was organised by Anglican churches on a voluntary basis. While the older boys in the village were catered for by the Grammar School, there was a need for a building for the education of girls and infants. This was provided in 1850 with the opening of a new school next to the vicarage, paid for by funds raised in the parish. Initially called the New Industrial School, it had two classrooms, the larger for older girls, the smaller for infants of both sexes. Standards in its early years were not high but by the end on the century consistently good reports were being received from government inspectors. An increase in numbers led to the appointment in 1905 of a second teacher to help the overworked headmistress and her assistant. During the 1920s the school roll stabilised at around 60 children. In 1939 work started on a major extension to the school in readiness for the transfer of the boys from the Grammar School which was scheduled to close. On October 1st 1940 the two schools amalgamated to form the Bolton-le-Sands Church of England Mixed School. Eventually, even this enlarged school was to prove inadequate for the growing population of the village and in 1967 a brand new school was opened on Mount Pleasant Lane.

RULES

For the Management of the GIRLS' INDUSTRIAL SCHOOL for the District of Bolton, Slyne-with-Hest, and Nether Kellet.

THE FOLLOWING RULES HAVE BEEN AGREED UPON BY THE COMMITTEE OF MANAGEMENT :—

I.

That useful Needlework of all kinds, plain Knitting, Reading, Bible Lessons, Writing, and Arithmetic, be the first and principal things taught in the School.

II.

That regular attendance of the Scholars be required from a Quarter before Nine to Twelve in the Morning, and from One to a Quarter-past Four in the Afternoon.

III.

The Payments to be weekly, and in advance, every Monday morning, according to the following Scale :—for the Child of every Labourer or poor person, recommended by an Annual Subscriber, *One Penny* per Week, for Reading, Knitting, and Sewing, with an additional Half-penny for writing on the Slate, or One Penny for writing on Paper.

That for all other Children, the Mistress be at liberty to make her own charge, subject to the approval of the Committee.

IV.

That Copy Books be paid for by the Scholars, when they receive them, at cost price—Pens, Ink, and Pencils will be found by the Committee.

V.

That Coals will be provided by the Committee, and each Scholar will be required to pay Sixpence for the Season, viz., Threepence on the first of October, and Threepence on the re-opening of the School after the Christmas Holidays.

VI.

That the Holidays be Two Weeks at Midsummer, and Two Weeks at Christmas.

Parents desiring further Information, are requested to apply through the District Visitors.

Young Boys may be admitted not above Eight Years' old.

These rules for the running of the school at Crosshill when it opened would surely give today's pupils pause for thought. Girls in particular would be affronted by the narrowness of the curriculum, with Needlework and Knitting deemed to be of prime importance and all would be appalled by the shortness of the holidays. The cost of materials was obviously a determining factor in learning to write and some children may have struggled when not even the extra halfpenny for the slate could be found that week.

This card, sent to Oldham in 1910, shows children outside Crosshill School with Hawkshead Farmhouse and The Nook in the background. Their presence in the road would become increasingly hazardous as the volume of traffic grew, although it took until 1937 before a safe playground was provided. Clearly visible in the picture is the sign of Thomas Brighton, House Decorator, who lived in the cottage next to the school with his wife Emma and six children.

Headmistress Miss Whittaker and assistant teachers Miss Brearley and Miss Taberner help line up the children for a photograph on the road between the school and the Blue Anchor Hotel in 1908. One little boy doesn't seem very interested in proceedings, preferring to sit on his own underneath the shop window.

This picture of the Infants and their teacher Miss French dates from about 1930. Dorothy Nelson started at Crosshill School in April 1928 aged four years and seven months. She remembers sitting two to a desk facing the blackboard and writing with pens whose nibs were dipped in inkwells set into the desk. Lessons included Arithmetic, Drawing, English, Geography, History and Scripture. There was also Nature Study with walks around the lanes and down to the shore. *'The classroom had windows too high to see out of. There was a big fireplace but it wasn't very effective and we would huddle round it for warmth on cold mornings. It was not until 1936 that central heating was installed and electric lighting two years later. The toilets were outside with only a cold tap for washing. At playtime we would play rounders in the yard, which was very cobbly, or go skipping in the road. I would walk home for a meal at lunchtime which lasted from 12 noon to 1.30 pm. There was church every Friday morning with a holiday on Ascension Day, half a day off for Shrove Tuesday and a whole day off for Morecambe Carnival'.*

Now a residence, this building on Kellet Lane was once a Catholic Elementary School. Until it opened in 1895 Catholic children received their education in the village's Anglican schools. The new school was financed by Miss Anne Coulston of Hawkshead House who also paid for its furnishings and those of the adjacent schoolhouse. The *Lancaster Guardian* was impressed, stating that the buildings 'are well lighted and ventilated, and already so well furnished with all the newest school apparatus and furniture, that they deserve to be set down as a model school and schoolhouse.' Designed to accommodate 60 boys and girls, the number on roll averaged around 40 for the first three decades with half the children coming from outside Bolton-le-Sands. In general, the school followed a similar curriculum to the other schools in the village, introducing new subjects such as cookery and swimming as this became possible. A steady rise in numbers during the 1930s began to put pressure on space although, according to HMI reports, a good standard of education was maintained. Further increases in the post-war period led to classes being held in the parish hall and the schoolhouse and it was eventually accepted that larger premises were needed. Because many of the children travelled from other areas, a site in Carnforth was chosen as being more convenient, and in 1967 staff and pupils were relocated to the newly built Our Lady of Lourdes School on Kellet Road next to the Catholic church.

Smiling children pose for the camera outside the Victoria Home for Girls in 1910. Following a short-lived existence as a private girls' school, Red Bank House on the shore was offered free of rent to the Church of England's Waifs and Strays Society by Mrs Peacock of Hest Bank Lodge who also donated £120 towards its furnishings. It began life as a children's home in late 1897 with fifteen girls in the care of an experienced matron, Miss H.M. Garratt. The aim of the Society was 'to receive destitute children and to provide for their care' rather than let them be sent to the workhouse. The Victoria Home was officially opened the following July. At the close of the dedication service Canon Beechley, vicar of Holy Trinity Church, explained that it had been so named by the 'express permission of Queen Victoria in commemoration of her Diamond Jubilee'. After the ceremony tea was served in a marquee in the garden, with musical accompaniment from a military band. Situated on the edge of Morecambe Bay the Victoria Home provided a healthy contrast to the deprived inner city areas where most of the girls had previously lived, and it was hoped that they would be 'strengthened by the balmy breezes of the sea'. The Victoria Home closed in 1920 when Red Bank House was sold by the owner and the Society did not have sufficient funds to purchase it.

Another small private school for girls was to be found at The Cottage, a house next to the canal on Packet Hill. Its principal for much of the last quarter of the 19th century was Mrs Mary Masheder. On her death in 1892 several 'old girls' combined to place a stained-glass window of St Michael in the tower of the parish church in 'affectionate remembrance' of their old teacher. The house was then bought by solicitor Herbert Wilson from Crosthwaite, near Kendal. The lady standing at the front door, photographed in 1905, is probably Helen Wesley who was employed as a nurse to look after Mr Wilson's two young children. It remains a private residence today, easily recognisable in its coat of pink paint.

Situated on fields at the southern edge of the village, Burnley Camp School was the brainchild of Dr J.W. Clegg, mayor of Burnley in 1925. He organised a fund for the provision of a holiday camp where children from the heavily industrialised urban areas of East Lancashire could experience fresh air and beautiful countryside. By August 1926 the buildings were ready and early the following month the first group of 25 girls arrived from Burnley by special charabanc. Children usually came for two weeks and enjoyed a wide range of outdoor activities which would not have been possible back home. In this view of the site taken from the canal towpath, the long building on the right contained the dormitories while the one on the left had rooms for teaching and dining plus accommodation for the permanent staff. The school continued until 1972 when the land was sold for residential development.

Burnley Camp School, Bolton-le-Sands

BURNLEY HOLIDAY CAMP

Each of Burnley Camp School's two wooden dormitories could sleep 25 girls or boys in what appear to be rather Spartan conditions. In between was a brick building in which slightly more comfortable facilities were provided for visiting teachers. The dining room was used as a classroom if the weather was bad but lessons, as far as possible, were held in the open air.

While Burnley Camp School had its own staff, some teachers also accompanied their children for the fortnight. One sent this card to her niece in Southport in 1934: *'We have been here just a week but it seems much longer than that. I expect the next week will simply fly. I have enjoyed the change very much but believe me it is a full time job. The girls are really enjoying themselves – you ought to see the quantity of food they put away, one wonders where they put it all. We have lessons in a morning, Drama, Nature, Sketching, Games, Country Dancing and excursions along the shore and in the country. Yesterday we climbed Warton Crag. You ought to have heard the cheers when I arrived at the top.'*

Burnley Camp School, Bolton-le-Sands.

Bolton le Sands.

JUVENILE BALL
BOLTON-LE-SANDS.

MR. HOLME

Begs most respectfully to announce to his friend and the public
of Bolton-le-Sands and its vicinity, that his

BALL

WILL TAKE PLACE AT

Mrs. Carter's, Blue Anchor Hotel,

On Thursday, the 24th day of October, 1861.

PROGRAMME.—Part 1.

Promanade March and Contre Dance	Lady's Hornpipe, by the Misses Jackson and Bleasdale.
Lady's Hornpipe by Miss Bibby, Queen of the Ball.	Quadrilles, the Lancers.
Scotch Fours, Large Class.	Gentleman's Hornpipe, Master M. Holme.
Gentleman's Hornpipe, Master E. Jackson.	Schottische.
Polka, Large Class.	Lady's Hornpipe, by the Misses Bleasdale and Shuttleworth.
Lady's Hornpipe, by Miss Butler.	Contre Dance, cross hands, Small Class.
Swiss Contre Dance.	Gentleman's Hornpipe, Master Shaw.
Gentleman's Hornpipe, Master T. Langton.	Sailor's Hornpipe by Master M. Holme.
Lady's Hornpipe, with the hoop, Miss Bleasdale.	Lady's Hornpipe with the hoop, by Miss Jackson.
Cotillion, old style, Small Class.	Valse and Galop.

AN INTERVAL OF TWENTY MINUTES.

PART 2.

Circassian Circle.	Gentleman's Hornpipe, by Master Jackson.
Lady's Hornpipe by Miss Leeming.	Garland Dance.
Scotch Fours, Small Class.	Lady's Hornpipe, with hoop, by Miss E. Shuttleworth.
Gentleman's Hornpipe, Master R. Miller.	Polka, Small Class.
Quadrilles, Paine's.	Lady's Hornpipe, by the Misses Carter and Hudson.
Lady's Hornpipe, by Misses Shuttleworth and Ratcliff.	The Figure Dance, Prince of Wales.
La Varsoviana.	Gentleman's Hornpipe, Master Hodgson.

TO CONCLUDE WITH THE

VOLUNTEERS' MARCH & DANCE.

Dancing to commence at Six o'clock Precisely.

Tickets to be had of Mr. HOLME, or at the Bar of the above Hotel.

The Room will be at the service of the Visitors after the Juveniles have finished.

NEVATT, PRINTER, 127, CHURCH STREET, LANCASTER.

Situated next to Holy Trinity Church on Crosshill, the Blue Anchor is the oldest inn/hotel in Bolton-le-Sands, dating back to 1706. Such hostelries were important centres of village life, albeit mainly for men, where cards, dominoes and skittles could be played and conversations washed down with glasses of beer. On this card from around 1910 the Blue Anchor's landlord, John Reynolds, is advertising 'Wines and Spirits of the Best Quality; Mild and Bitter Ales; Luncheons, Dinners & Teas; Large Parties Catered For'. Large parties could be accommodated in a spacious, first-floor room above the stables at the back of the hotel. Known as the Assembly Room it was used for various village functions, especially dances and balls such as that shown above from 1861, held under the auspices of landlady Mary Carter. One rather different use of the room occurred in 1880 when the parish church was closed for repairs and the Bishop of Manchester gave permission 'for the performance of Divine Service and for publication of Banns and solemnisation of Marriages therein'.

The Blue Anchor was a popular stopping-off point for horse-drawn charabancs from Lancaster and Morecambe taking parties out to enjoy the countryside. In this scene from 1905 several carriages have pulled up to give their passengers (dressed in what appears to be 'Sunday best') a chance to stretch their legs and take some refreshment. The plaque on the wall to the left of the hotel entrance is that of the Cyclists Touring Club. Founded in 1878, the CTC had over 60,000 members by 1900, a reflection of the increasing enthusiasm for the bicycle which offered its owner fresh air, personal mobility and access to the countryside.

Iames Bibby Built these Houses in 1745

Crosshill once had two inns. Separated from the Blue Anchor only by Bennison's shop, the Black Bull (and its neighbouring house) was built in 1745 by James Bibby, a wealthy local man who is thought to have made his money in the West Indies trade. Although the words 'James Bibby built these houses in 1745' are inscribed on the lintel, it is not clear whether one of the 'houses' was originally an inn or became the Black Bull some time later. The inn was a popular meeting place for local farmers and traders when negotiating deals and was also often used for property auctions. This early photograph from around 1890 shows landlord William Clarke with his wife Mary and son John.

By 1904 the Black Bull Hotel had acquired a large sign advertising 'YATE'S MANCHESTER ALES & STOUT' and a smart new horse-drawn charabanc. William Clarke is still shown as landlord although by this time he was in his mid-seventies. It is likely that his son John, sitting on the carriage, would be helping to run the hotel as well as offering excursions to holidaymakers.

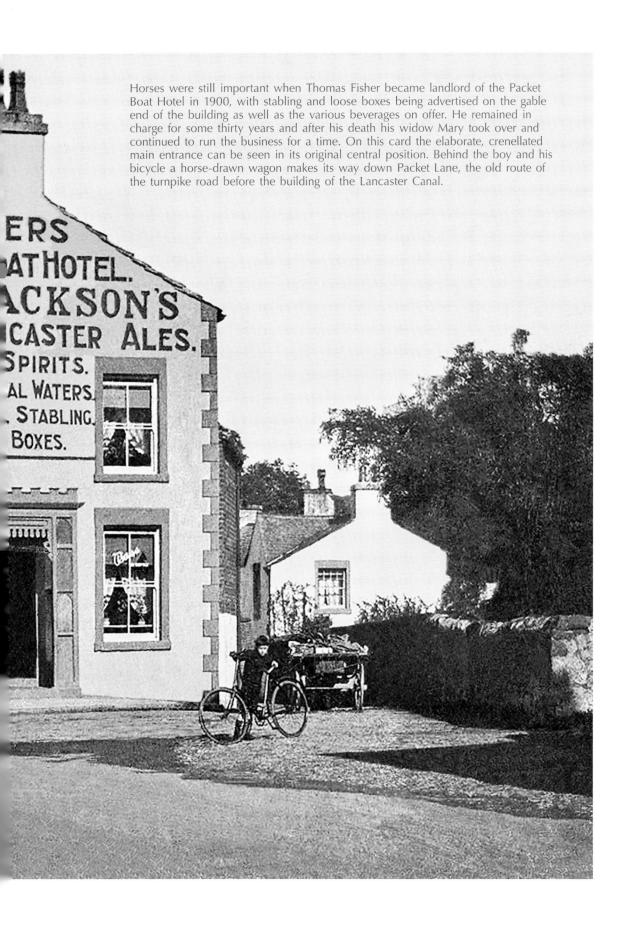

Horses were still important when Thomas Fisher became landlord of the Packet Boat Hotel in 1900, with stabling and loose boxes being advertised on the gable end of the building as well as the various beverages on offer. He remained in charge for some thirty years and after his death his widow Mary took over and continued to run the business for a time. On this card the elaborate, crenellated main entrance can be seen in its original central position. Behind the boy and his bicycle a horse-drawn wagon makes its way down Packet Lane, the old route of the turnpike road before the building of the Lancaster Canal.

In addition to its main inns Bolton-le-Sands, like many villages, also had a number of beer houses. Under the Beer Act of 1830 people were permitted to sell alcohol in their own homes, usually in the front parlour. Often profits were so high that owners were able to buy the house next door to live in and turn the rooms of their former home into bars and lounges for customers. Some applied for new licences and became bona fide pubs. One such was the Fisherman's Arms at the northern end of Main Road, known locally as the 'Old Jerry'. This photograph from 1900, shows it separated from Laurel House by three terraced cottages. In 1903, George Hornby, landlord of the Fisherman's Arms, received planning permission to demolish the cottages and build a new hotel. Sadly, no mention is made of what happened to the evicted families of John Hutchinson (ironworks labourer), George Orliff (agricultural labourer) and George Huddleston (coachman). The original intention was to retain the title Fisherman's Arms for the new building but on its completion the name Royal Hotel was adopted.

When the Royal Hotel opened in 1904 the old Fisherman's Arms was converted into a café which can be seen in this unposted card. The cars suggest a date sometime in the 1920s and indicate the growing importance of the Royal Hotel to the motorist. As cars and coaches became more common the Royal gradually acquired a reputation as a stopping place for travellers, helped by its favourable location on the main road north. Coaches from Morecambe and Blackpool en route to the Lake District would call in for morning coffee and order meals for their return in late afternoon. To accommodate the increase in vehicle numbers the adjoining café was demolished while additional parking was provided on land across the road.

Shops and Services

After the Black Bull Hotel closed, the building re-opened as the Black Bull Café providing luncheons, dinners and teas and selling pure ices and American drinks. A few years later it became the Bolton-le-Sands branch of the Co-operative Society. This looked after the village's grocery needs for several decades before closing in the mid 1970s. It was attractive to customers who liked its 'own brand' products of proven reliability at competitive prices. The writer of this card, sent to Warrington in September 1919, was beginning a holiday at Crosshill Cottage next door to the café: *'We reached here at 1 o'clock and enjoyed a good dinner. This is a picture of the house we are staying at and we shall enjoy ourselves if the weather keeps fine.'*

Sandwiched between the Blue Anchor and the Black Bull was E.M. Bennison's grocery and confectionery shop, a great favourite with children from the village schools. A spinster originally from Catterick in Yorkshire, Elizabeth Bennison lived above the business with her nephew and two nieces. Richard Lee was landlord of the Black Bull next door when this card was sent in 1912 and was still listed as such in *Bulmer's Directory* a year later. However, the Black Bull must have closed soon afterwards as another card, posted in late 1913, shows the building with all the inn signs removed.

Cuts of meat hang in the window of Ralph Millner's butcher's shop on Main Road. Several generations of Millners were butchers in the village, starting out at premises now occupied by the Packet Boat Hotel's car park. While the hygiene of the shop was probably acceptable for the time, the absence of refrigerated counters and the propensity of glass to trap the sun make the sight less appealing to modern eyes. Pigs, lambs and the occasional cow were slaughtered in a building to the rear of the shop, not always in the most humane ways. A bearded Ralph Millner stands in the centre of the picture taken around 1925. His son, Thomas Houghton Millner, on the extreme left, inherited the business and ran it until his retirement in 1950. Since ceasing to be a butcher's, the shop has had several changes of use including a hairdresser, newsagent, bakery, haberdashery and pie shop.

Next door to Millner's shop was the Rose Café and bakery, owned for many years by Alfred and Amy Steele. It was already established as a café when they took over the property in 1931 but prior to that had been a coachbuilder's works. According to the 1901 Census the works was being run by Isaac Lawrence with help from his fifteen year old son William. Isaac had four other children, including an older daughter whose occupation was given as confectioner and baker – perhaps it was she who originally opened a café. Even with a family of seven, Rose Cottage, as it was then called, still had sufficient room to provide accommodation for two boarders. The Steeles gradually developed a thriving business with a bakery and shop and a café large enough to cater for weddings and funerals. Two vans also distributed their bread and cakes over a wide radius, to places such as Slyne and Hest Bank, Carnforth, the Kellets, Arkholme and Whittington. In 1954 the café was closed and the shop enlarged, later becoming a Mace mini-supermarket. After the bakery shut down, the family continued to run the shop until its sale in 1986. Today it is a Spar convenience store.

MAIN ROAD, BOLTON LE SANDS.

The datestone in McGaffigan's yard reveals the property to be over 300 years old and first owned by George Preston, an innkeeper by profession, and his wife Alice. The buildings are now much altered but their layout still resembles an inn yard. A smithy was certainly in operation in the early 19th century, being run by a local blacksmith called John Statter. In 1828, unable to repay a sizeable debt, he was forced to sell the blacksmith's shop and adjacent cottages. The sale document gives the name of the buyer as Richard Sparling Berry, a wealthy bachelor of Bolton Lodge, who paid Statter the sum of £430. In 1901 five families were living in the yard's cottages including blacksmith Anthony Wrathall, his wife and their six children. The other occupants were a fisherman, an ironworks labourer, a widow and a gravel pit labourer – altogether, with their families, a total of 22 persons.

Patrick McGaffigan bought the smithy in 1919 after coming over from Ireland and working as a blacksmith in Morecambe. At that time, when the horse was the principal means of transport, the blacksmith was the essential village craftsman. Apart from shoeing horses he also forged the metal rims for cart and carriage wheels and made and repaired iron agricultural equipment. Patrick was helped in the smithy by two of his sons, Jack and Tommy who eventually took over the business. They are young boys in this 1928 photograph, to the left of their father who poses for the camera as he fits a horse's shoe. As tractors replaced horses the smithy survived because it diversified into other areas and today concentrates on decorative wrought iron work and making parts for other blacksmiths. Remarkably, it is still in the same family. Paul Modley, great-grandson of Patrick, bought the business in 1986 and is now helped by his two sons – the sixth generation of McGaffigans, if not in actual name.

The McGaffigan family was also closely associated with the local fire brigade with Jack being appointed leader at its formation in 1939 and Tommy later becoming his deputy. A light portable pump with ancillary equipment was obtained and kept in a garage next to the Catholic presbytery in Kellet Lane.

Five years later an 18th-century barn on Main Road was converted into a fire station with a small control room. It was able to accommodate bigger and better fire engines – although the Bedford engine shown here found it rather a tight fit. Fire calls were received at McGaffigan's 24 hours a day and a siren on the roof of the smithy would alert the firemen, together with an alarm bell in each fireman's house. Although small in size, the Bolton-le-Sands station was well respected within the service and in 1946 won a prestigious trophy which was competed for by all stations between Crewe and Carlisle. In 1968 the firemen were able to give up their cramped conditions in the centre of the village and move to a purpose-built, two-bay fire station on Bye-Pass Road. After the old barn was vacated it became a branch of the Nat West Bank and is now a private residence.

One unusual service to be found in the village was that provided by the self-styled Professor Ray who lived at Prospect House next to Packet Bridge. Described in a 1913 trade directory as a 'Medical Electrician', J. F. Ray produced his own promotional postcards which showed him in authoritative pose, his face almost obscured by a luxuriant moustache. He was more than likely one of the many quack medical practitioners of the time who claimed that electricity could cure almost every conceivable ailment. His principal method of treatment consisted of attaching electrodes from a battery to the body (especially the head) of a patient, then varying the type and intensity of the current as was thought appropriate. One wonders whether the effects of such therapy were beneficial or resulted in lasting damage!

PROFESSOR. RAY.

Situated halfway down Packet Hill, Speight's was a draper's and hosier's which also sold toys and fancy goods. The attention of the boater-hatted gentleman seems drawn to a display of postcards in the shop window. It is quite possible that a card such as this, dating from 1906, was available for purchase in the shop. The other figure in the picture is walking past an old barn which became a garage in the 1920s and in the late 1950s was converted by butcher John Bowker to increase the size of his shop and provide living accommodation above.

William Hayton Whiteside stands proudly outside his newsagent's and tobacconist's on Packet Hill in 1918. He ran the shop until 1940 after which it became the village Post Office. Reflected in the window, above the row of glass jars, is the roof and chimney of Jessamine Cottage opposite. As a newsagent, William Hayton Whiteside was often in receipt of postcards in connection with his business and one example from September 1920 serves to epitomise the convenience of this means of communication at the time. Rather than walk the short distance to Packet Hill from his house on Grange View, Mr William Bracewell preferred to send a card with the request to *'please discontinue sending Daily Mail until further notice.'*

Before he started his Newsagent's shop on Packet Hill, William Hayton Whiteside, pictured outside the Post Office in 1910, was a farmer and part-time postman. The use of bicycles for mail deliveries had been officially introduced by the Post Office in 1897 in response to the increase in telegram traffic.

A white-bearded Thomas Wildman, his wife Fanny and an assortment of children pose for the camera outside the village Post Office on Main Road in 1905. The Wildmans lived 'above the shop' with their grandson and nephew, both of whom worked as clerks for the Post Office. The notice above the door informs customers that this is a 'Postal Telegraph Office' and a 'Post Office for Money Order, Savings Bank, Parcel Post, Telegraph, Insurance and Annuity Business'. After serving the village for some fifty years from this building, the Post Office moved to its present location on Packet Hill in 1940.

Resplendent in a floral-patterned dress, local businesswoman Mrs Ribchester sits outside her recently completed Cosy Café. Built of wooden boards with an asphalt roof, it was situated on the bend at the bottom of Packet Hill – sadly to prove an unfortunate location. Having received planning permission in May 1922 the Cosy Café was fated to enjoy only a relatively brief existence, falling victim to the new bypass road four years later.

A few doors down from the Royal Hotel was the grocery shop and bakery of Mary Bell. She was renowned for the quality of her cakes which were much in demand both in the village and further afield. A postcard received in 1907 by Elizabeth Whiteside (who lived almost opposite the shop) from her niece contained the request *'If you come to Lancaster will you bring me a cake from Mary Bell. Yours was very nice.'*

MOSSDALE CAFE, BOLTON LE SANDS.

Mossdale Café occupied one half of the building on Main Road which is now Trung's Chinese Restaurant. In the 1930s it was owned by Walter Haines who also had a baker's and confectioner's shop at the side of the café. On this card he had been succeeded by George Salter who ran the business with the help of his son Clifford. Known locally as the 'Muffin Man', Clifford would travel round the village selling muffins and other baked items from a hand cart.

The builder and contractor John William Cottam had his base in Town End in an old barn, since replaced by two houses. He built a number of properties on Broadlands Drive and Slyne Road, including the Merry Kettle Café (below) and also worked in Warton and Nether Kellet. Opposite the barn were the greenhouses of Town End Nursery, one of several market gardens in the village before and after World War II, none of which survived the housing developments of the 1960s and 1970s.

TOWNEND, BOLTON-LE-SANDS

The Merry Kettle was a popular café on Slyne Road identified by its distinctive emblem, a large, steaming kettle with a smiling face mounted above the doorway. At the back were hard tennis courts for hire at one shilling an hour, a facility which gave the building its original name of the Court Café. It had become the Merry Kettle when this card was sent in 1941, the message reading *'Have just finished having lunch at the café on the card, it was real, a knife and fork do, we have walked all the way from Morecambe partly along the canal bank.'* Today, the traditional English fare of the Merry Kettle has been replaced by the more exotic Eastern cuisine on offer at Ricky's Cantonese restaurant.

Merry Kettle Cafe, Slyne Road, Bolton-le-Sands.

Pictured here in the early 1960s, the Willow Tree Café was located on Bye-Pass Road, near the junction with St Michael's Lane. For many years it operated as a transport café, a convenient place for long-distance lorry drivers to break their journeys north or south. However, with the opening of the M6 motorway around Lancaster in 1960 this trade fell away and the Willow Tree became more of a traditional 'three-course dinner' type of establishment. This put it in competition with the long-established XL Café almost opposite, easily recognisable by the large letters X and L painted on its roof. Capable of seating 120 diners, the XL Café had the reputation of providing the best quality meals in the village and was particularly noted for its Sunday lunches. It was sold in 1968 and turned into a Little Chef Restaurant. Today a small housing development occupies the site while across the road the Willow Tree remains in business, albeit under its new identity of The Far Pavilion Indian Restaurant.

Houses

Rose Cottage and Primrose Cottage used to be the first houses encountered when entering Bolton-le-Sands from the south. In 1901 they were occupied respectively by widow Mary Willman and her daughter Isobella, and stonemason Allan Bell, his wife Annie and niece Emma. They continued as two separate residences until 1957 when Leslie and Marian Rigg, then living in Rose Cottage, bought the neighbouring property and knocked through to create one larger dwelling. During the conversion work a connecting door was discovered, leading to speculation that the building might originally have been a farmhouse in the pre-canal age.

Bolton-le-Sands.

Church Cottages lie at the end of a short track between Holy Trinity Church and its main graveyard. Built in 1672 by John and Jane Hall, they are two of the oldest surviving dwellings in the village. For several generations the cottages were owned by members of the Hodgson family, John Hodgson, a cordwainer (shoemaker), having bought them for £175 in 1838. At the time he was a tenant in one of the properties which then belonged to Ann Todd, whose late husband had been Master at the Free Grammar School. William, the great grandson of John Hodgson, was still living in number 1, Church Cottages when this card was produced in the early 1920s but seems to have been the first Hodgson not to follow the family trade, earning his living as a music teacher. In recent years both cottages have been extended with number 2 creating an additional room from the adjacent pig sty and peat house.

The Nook contains several old properties of which the most impressive is Hawkshead Farmhouse pictured on the left. It was built in 1665 by Richard Chapman whose initials are cut into the lintel above the door. Constructed of sandstone and limestone rubble with sandstone dressings and a slate roof, it has rebated mullioned windows with continuous drip courses on the ground and first floors and is of sufficient architectural importance to warrant a Grade II* listing. Like several other farmhouses in the village it is no longer at the heart of a working farm and the fields it still owns are used mainly for horses.

The Nook, Bolton-le-Sands.

Bolton-le-Sands.

Further up The Nook, at its junction with Ancliffe Lane, is Jenkinson's Farmhouse which is late Georgian in age. The Jenkinsons had been associated with Bolton-le-Sands since the 16th century and owned much land in the village, including this farm at the top of The Nook. In the 1860s it was being run by Henry Clarkson, a prominent Roman Catholic. At this time there was no provision in the village for Catholics to worship and Henry Clarkson offered a detached barn next to his farmhouse for this purpose. Miss Anne Coulston of Hawkshead House paid for the barn's conversion and it served as a chapel from 1868 until the completion of the Church of St Mary of the Angels in 1884. Henry Clarkson's son Thomas took over the farm from his father and it remained in the family until the early 1980s.

Winding its way down from the village centre, St Michael's Lane passes by the terrace of houses which constitutes St Michaels' Grove. The houses, with their long, narrow rear gardens, occupy the site of an old brewery. Until the end of the 19th century barley was widely grown on local farms and much of it was converted into malt which was used to make beer. Two malt kilns were located in Town End but the most successful was at St Michael's Well where a brewery business, operated by James Hull and Sons, continued in operation until its closure and demolition in the mid 1890s. The bypass road was still four years in the future when this card was posted in 1922.

ST MICHAEL'S WELL BREWERY,

BOLTON LE SANDS,

BREWERS, MALTSTERS & SPIRIT MERCHANTS.

BOLTON-LE-SANDS

St MICHAELS WELL HOUSE,
BOLTON-LE-SANDS, CARNFORTH.

Next to the canal and detached from the other houses of St Michael's Grove, is Well House, so named because it stands next to St Michael's Well, one of several holy wells in the village. Records exist of baptisms being conducted at the well in the 18th century as many poor people could not afford the baptismal fee charged by the church for this service. Elsewhere in the village was a well dedicated to St Patrick, another to St Nicholas (the patron saint of sailors and fishermen) and a Monks' Well on land which belonged to Furness Abbey. Two of the people pictured in the garden are probably Herbert Procter and his wife Jane who lived at Well House in the early years of the 20th century. He was a civil engineer and surveyor by profession and sufficiently well off to employ a governess for his three daughters, plus a cook and a housemaid. In later years Well House became a boarding house and then a doctor's surgery before reverting to a private residence.

This pair of small cottages once stood behind and below what is now Packet Bridge Fish and Chip shop. In 1901 one was lived in by bricklayer John Helman, his wife and two young daughters, the other by fisherman Richard Davis and his sons Charles, a shoemaker, and Richard, a labourer.

Darwen House, in the centre of this view of Main Road, was once a farmhouse with a barn attached (now Darwen Cottage). In 1911, the year this card was posted to Stockport, it was the home of William Windle who had recently retired after 27 years of service as Master at the Free Grammar School. On the other side of the gap (now filled by the library) the first house was the police station at the beginning of the 20th century. All the iron railings fronting the properties have since disappeared, probably sacrificed in wartime to be melted down for their metal. As well as a daughter, William and Harriet Windle had two sons, John and Cyril. When the First World War broke out they enlisted in the army together, were then sent to France together and, poignantly, died together in September 1916 at the Battle of the Somme – a long way from home.

When this card was sent in 1905 the terrace of six small houses on Main Road had been in existence for eleven years. Built by local architect Richard Bibby Jackson of Lane Head House, they were then occupied by the families of a stonemason, a sawyer, an agricultural labourer, a shoemaker and two railway workers. Though the occasional vehicle might pass through the village it was still possible for people to hold conversations in the middle of the road in perfect safety.

Mature trees, including an impressive Araucarian Pine, flank The Chestnuts Hotel on a card from the late 1930s. Although then a hotel, it had begun life as a gentleman's residence in about 1870, having been built for eminent local surgeon Dr William Jackson and originally called Chestnut Villa. The house stood in extensive grounds and was one of several large properties within close proximity to each other at the northern end of the village. Its upmarket neighbours included Laurel House, Waterloo Cottage, Croftlands and the late-Georgian Westbrook Lodge with its symmetrical façade and elegant wrought-iron balcony over the front entrance. In recent years The Chestnuts has been a residential care home for the elderly and is now a children's home with the new name of Woodlands.

Directly across Main Road from Chestnut Villa was Laurel House. In December 1905 its owner, Thomas Kirkbride, used this card of his home to send Christmas greetings to his friends Alderman and Mrs Snowden of Heysham Road, Morecambe. To the left of Laurel House is the corner of its neighbour, Waterloo Cottage. In 1880 William Towers, the newly ordained Pastor of Carnforth Congregational Church, became the tenant of Laurel House and was given permission to start a mission in the loft above the stable. The services aroused a certain amount of anger among some of the residents of the village as Nonconformists were then still viewed with suspicion. Those attending were warned that they would be 'marked men' and their comings and goings were closely observed from Chestnut Villa opposite.

The large Victorian house known as Croftlands occupied an elevated position on the corner of Mill Lane and Main Road. Standing in 1.6 acres of landscaped gardens it was reached by a sweeping, tree-lined drive. At the time of the 1901 Census Croftlands was owned by Richard Langley, a wealthy ironmonger from the Potteries, who lived there with his wife and daughter. After changing hands it was put up for auction in 1949 at the Royal Hotel, Bolton-le-Sands. The writer of the sale brochure obviously had a certain class of purchaser in mind, emphasising the opportunities for golf, fishing and yachting and noting that 'excellent rough shooting and wildfowling are available' and that 'there are fox, stag and otter hunts in the surrounding district'. In 1954 it was on the market again and was bought by Ernald Rawlinson, a mill owner from Rossendale.

Ernald Rawlinson and his wife Margaret lived at Croftlands until 1965 when they decided that the house was too large for them and, rather than move elsewhere, opted to have it demolished and replaced by a modern bungalow on the same site. Very little of the building was left when this photograph was taken. Following Ernald Rawlinson's death in 1992 (Margaret had predeceased him) the remaining grounds and adjacent field were sold for housing and today the land is occupied by a cul-de-sac of 'executive homes' known as Croftlands Gardens.

PARK CRESCENT-BOLTON-L. SANDS.

Posted to Nelson in 1915 this card shows houses
in Park Crescent, now Whin Grove. The slopes of
Thwaite Brow in the background were then much less
wooded and had a park-like appearance – hence the
original name of the road. On the right is a lodging
house, one of three built in 1901; the middle one of
these was later demolished and replaced by a more
modern building in a similar style.

A winter scene looking from Thwaite Brow across snow-covered fields to Hawkshead House in the distance. The impressive mansion was built in 1856 by wealthy banker John Coulston who had bought the Hawkshead estate a few years earlier. Once the house was finished John was joined by his sister Anne who inherited the property on her brother's death in 1866. Anne was a devout Catholic and provided the money for the Church of St Mary of the Angels at Crosshill and the Catholic school on Kellet Lane.

By the time this card was sent in 1907 Anne Couston had died and been succeeded at Hawkshead House by her great-nephew Henry Knowles, a barrister and local Justice of the Peace. He lived there with his wife Mary, stepdaughter and two sons, having adopted the name of Coulston after he moved in. The large house with its classical façade required an equally large staff to maintain it. Five domestic servants looked after the inside tasks while several gardeners were employed to keep the extensive grounds neat and tidy. The two entrance lodges provided accommodation for the coachmen and grooms who were responsible for the family's horses and carriages.

On special occasions the grounds of Hawkshead House would be opened to local people. In this picture villagers have dressed up in various costumes to celebrate George V's Silver Jubilee in 1935. A similar pageant took place two years later for the coronation of George VI.

CATINGDALE

Thortindale Villa (sometimes spelt Thortingdale) dates to around 1830 and was lived in by John Coulston until the early 1850s when he acquired the Hawkshead estate. Attached to the symmetrical main part of the house is a vaguely ecclesiastical annex which, it is said, John Coulston had adapted as a private chapel.

For many years Thortindale stood in a solitary location on the eastern side of the Lancaster Canal and was reached across this swivel bridge via a track from the coastal road, still the only access today.

SWIVEL BRIDGE
BOLTON-le-SANDS

When this card was sent in 1909 only two houses stood on the stretch of shore between the points where Pasture Lane and St Michael's Lane petered out into the salt marsh. The more distant house, then called Sandbank, was built in 1908 while the nearer one is much older, being marked on several early 19th-century maps. Originally known as Pastureland Cottage, it had been re-named Elmside and extended by the time of this photograph and now goes under the more mundane designation of 1, The Shore.

By the 1930s a certain amount of infilling had occurred between the two earlier properties and also beyond Sandbank to St Michael's Lane. Located next to the salt marsh and with little protection from the sea the houses were always susceptible to flooding at high tides, a danger that has been greatly reduced in recent years by the construction of a protective embankment parallel to the road.

THE SHORE, BOLTON-LE-SANDS.

Bay View Estate and Brow, Bolton-le-Sands.

The six pairs of semi-detached houses on Orchard Avenue pictured on this 1937 card were the first to be built on the Bay View Estate at the northern end of Bolton-le-Sands. Then in splendid isolation they marked the beginning of the inexorable spread of suburbia that would overtake the village in the ensuing decades.

After World War II there was a housing shortage and local authorities became more involved in building homes, especially for working-class people. At first building materials were in short supply but gradually new estates began to emerge, with increasing numbers of council houses being constructed. In Bolton-le-Sands the first houses on the Church Brow estate were completed in 1949 while at the other end of the village work had begun on another site between Main Road and the Lancaster Canal. This estate, known as Brookfield and shown here in 1950, was much smaller in size with the houses set out around an attractive open space.

Transport

The Lancaster Canal was constructed to transport coal north from the Lancashire coalfields and take limestone and farm produce back to the south of the county, earning it the soubriquet 'The Black and White Canal'. Here, two horses pull a barge round a curve in the canal just north of Packet Bridge. Large numbers of horses were in use in the early years of the 20th century and this resulted in a considerable amount of excrement. Manure from the many stables alongside the canal was collected in barges and sold as fertiliser to local farmers.

The coal barges of the Preston firm of W & J Turner were identified by girl's names and here *Ann* has tied up at Packet Boat wharf to unload some of her cargo. The barges were 14' 6" wide and 72' long with a capacity of 52 tons. They were nearly always horse-drawn, usually by a pair of horses, and progressed relatively slowly. The Packet Boat Hotel was named after much speedier craft. It was one of the stops for the fast, passenger-carrying boats which ran on the Lancaster Canal in the early 19th century between Preston and Kendal. The daily service opened on 11th May 1820 and took 14 hours to cover the 57 miles. Refreshments were available from a buffet between the first class fore-cabin and the larger, second class after-cabin. Fares for the whole trip were six shillings and four shillings respectively. By the mid 1830s the journey time had been halved by the introduction of two specially designed, iron-hulled 'express boats' called *Waterwitch* and *Swiftsure* which were pulled by pairs of horses changed every four miles. Despite this improved performance, the packet boats could not match the speed of the train and when the Lancaster and Carlisle railway reached Kendal on 21st September 1846 the packet boats were withdrawn from service. The cottage next to the Packet Boat is now part of the hotel while its neighbour on the left was demolished to create a car park.

This card, sent in 1921, shows a steamer towing four of W & J Turner's coal barges, with *Sarah* at the rear. However, there were problems with the steamer getting up the locks at Tewitfield and it was not long before the company reverted to horses which were used until business on the canal ceased in 1947.

THE BROW, BOLTON LE SANDS.

Thwaite Brow Bridge is one of four surviving original bridges in the village dating from the opening of the canal in 1797. All are Grade II listed and described in architectural parlance as having a 'Single semi-elliptical arch with projecting keystone' built with 'Large punched gritstone blocks' and a 'String course under a solid parapet with rounded coping'. Just beyond the bridge were a number of cinder ovens which were used to convert coal brought by the barges into cinders or coke, a hot-burning smokeless fuel much in demand by lime-burners and blacksmiths.

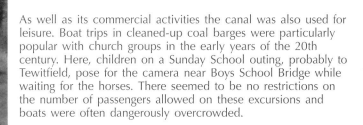

As well as its commercial activities the canal was also used for leisure. Boat trips in cleaned-up coal barges were particularly popular with church groups in the early years of the 20th century. Here, children on a Sunday School outing, probably to Tewitfield, pose for the camera near Boys School Bridge while waiting for the horses. There seemed to be no restrictions on the number of passengers allowed on these excursions and boats were often dangerously overcrowded.

A south-bound passenger train draws up at Bolton-le-Sands station on St Michael's Lane. The Lancaster & Carlisle Railway reached the village in 1846, greatly improving its links with the outside world. Local produce, especially perishable goods like fish, could be transported to markets more quickly and efficiently. The railway also gave people greater mobility, offering relatively cheap and easy access to larger centres of population for work and pleasure.

Ivatt Class locomotive 46400 waits at the north-bound platform of Bolton-le-Sands station, in a photograph probably from the late 1950s (the class was withdrawn after 1961). Today, nothing remains of the station nor the footbridge which once spanned the track. Perhaps because the railway was some distance from the centre of the village the station was never that well used, a fact which probably contributed to its closure in 1969.

By the time this card was produced the line was part of the London, Midland & Scottish Railway (LMS), one of the 'Big Four' companies created in 1923. The train has just passed under Mill Lane Bridge and is approaching Bolton-le-Sands station. The fields almost obscured by smoke from the engine are now covered in houses.

In the early 20th century the ownership of a horse was beyond the purse of most people and the carter was the main means of transport for a variety of loads. Sometimes farmers carried other people's goods as well as their own and frequently carters had other jobs. Deliveries tended to be local in nature but in Bolton-le-Sands longer distances could be covered by linking with the canal wharf or railway station. Watched by a curious little girl, carter Thomas Poulston pauses at a bend in Mill Lane, now the junction with Hawthorn Road. The large house in the distance is Croftlands which stood on the corner of Mill Lane and Main Road.

A steamroller struggles up Packet Hill on this card sent to Skegness in 1923. The message on the back was rather patronising about Bolton-le-Sands: *'We're having quite a decent time and will be home next Tuesday. This is to show you that civilisation here is still in the state when steam-rollers are used for rolling. They haven't reached the enlightened method of using them for traction only, and let the traffic do its own rolling!'*

Boltonlesands Village.

As well as carters and village roundsmen delivering bread and milk, groceries and household items on a regular basis, there were also carriers who went wherever they were paid. On this 1914 card a carrier poses with his wagon in Main Road outside Bolton Lodge. By this time most carriers had settled on a general type of wagon with a weatherproof cover which afforded some protection to both goods and passengers. The carriers themselves were, by law, obliged to walk alongside their horses in order to maintain control of them and thus prevent accidents.

THE PACKET BRIDGE. BOLTON LE SANDS.

By the mid 1920s traffic through Bolton-le-Sands had increased markedly, so much so that a policeman was employed to manage the vehicles crossing Packet Bridge. As it was impracticable to widen the bridge, Lancashire County Council took the decision to build a bypass road to divert through-traffic away from the centre of the village.

London Rd Bolton-le-Sands

A smartly dressed man chats to a woman at the bottom of Packet Hill where the main road north curves out of the village. The scene on this card, sent to Blackpool in 1924, gives no indication of the traffic congestion which prompted the construction of the bypass two years later and resulted in the demolition of Mrs Ribchester's Cosy Café.

Work on the bypass started on 1st February 1926 and involved the construction of a new stretch of road just under three-quarters of a mile in length, much of it on a raised embankment for which 50,000 cubic yards of soil was imported from the adjoining land. Here a bucket excavator is seen at work near Monkswell Farm. At the bottom right of the picture is the end of a rail track which was laid along the site to facilitate the transport of materials.

New Bridge - Bolton-le-Sands

To take the new carriageway over the Lancaster Canal at Town End a reinforced concrete bridge was built to replace its 1797 predecessor. Sadly for one house owner, the construction of a wider road required the demolition of his property at the end of Grange View.

OLD A

A view of the northern end of the bypass where it meets the bottom of Packet Hill. Although the card was posted in 1931 the photograph appears to be from a slightly earlier date, shortly after the road's completion.

The finished bypass was officially opened on 6th September 1928 at Town End where the new road made a fork with the old one. It had taken 31 months to build and had cost almost £50,000. This picture of the southern end was sent as a Christmas card to Hexham in 1930. The writer includes the observation that *'This part of Bolton has grown during the last 3 years'*, a reference to the houses which had recently been built along the eastern side of Slyne Road.

It

NEW ROAD & WARTON CRAG FROM TOWN END, BOLTON-LE-SANDS.

ROADS JUNCTION, BOLTON-LE-SANDS.

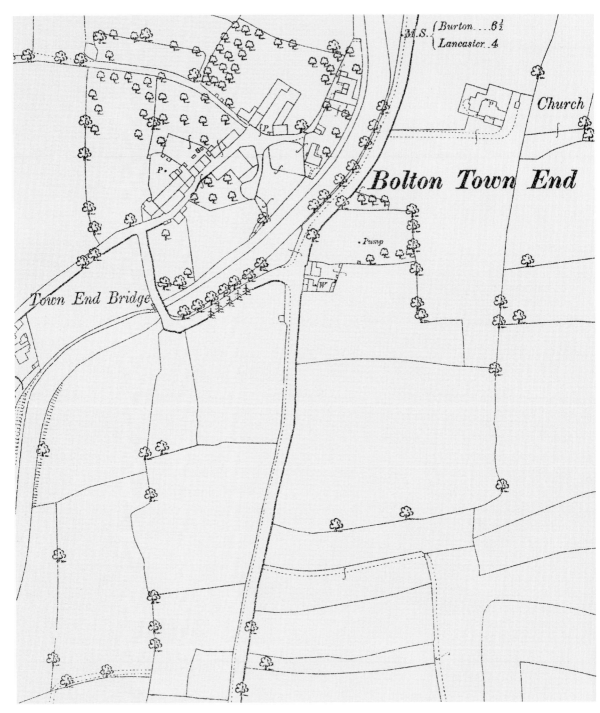

Bolton Town End in 1890 (above) and in 1930 (opposite).

Before the bypass the Lancaster Canal was crossed by a narrow bridge via a dog-legged approach from the main road opposite Rose Cottage. The houses of Grange View had yet to be built.

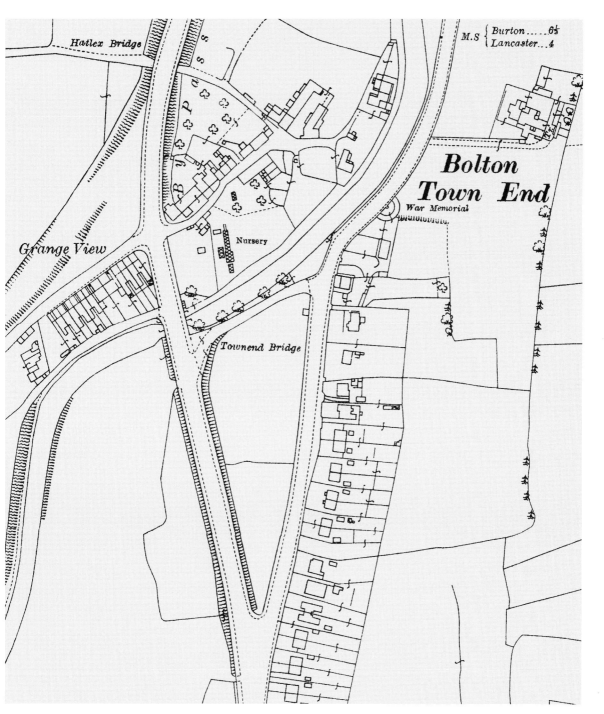

The following labels appear on the map:

Hatlex Bridge

By Pass

M.S { Burton 6½
Lancaster ... 4 }

Bolton Town End

War Memorial

Grange View

Nursery

Townend Bridge

The new, wider carriageway cut straight across the canal rising on a steady gradient from its junction with the old road leaving a triangle of land inbetween which, remarkably, still survives today as a green space. Semi-detached houses have appeared along the eastern side of Slyne Road, the beginnings of a ribbon development that would stretch a further half mile southwards. During the 1930s the fields between the bypass and the canal were replaced by the houses of Broadlands Drive.

TREE LANE, BOLTON-LE-SANDS

In this picture from around 1930, the new Town End Bridge can be seen through the trees at the far end of the narrow lane which links the old road with the bypass. Although aptly described as Tree Lane on the card, it is now officially known as Shady Lane and the trees are greatly reduced in number.

In May 1933 the bypass around Bolton-le-Sands was joined by a new coastal road which wound its way from Morecambe through Hest Bank to a point just north of Town End Bridge. The stretch of road shown on this card from 1934 is deserted save for a solitary motorcyclist passing between Mansefield on the right and the newly erected Fillit Petrol Station on the left. This was owned by Robert Chippendale and John Evans who also operated from the same premises as Electrical Engineers and radio contractors.

stal Road, Bolton-le-Sands

Once the bypass and the coastal road were joined at Town End a new signpost was required, the subject of this rather unimaginative postcard from 1935.

The Royal Garage of V. J. Swinglehurst on Main Road was one of the earliest to be established in the village. As well as serving petrol it offered a repair service and stocked a full range of motoring accessories. Victor Swinglehurst actively promoted his business by placing advertisements in several local publications. One such advert, in a parish magazine from 1924, informed readers that he supplied 'The leading makes of CARS and MOTOR CYCLES' and was 'Agent for Triumph, Raleigh, Royal Enfield, B.S.A., James, and Centaur Motor Cycles and Cycles'. There were 'Cars for Hire, day or night' with 'Weddings a Speciality'.

In the mid 1930s Bolton-le-Sands was well off for garages. In addition to Swinglehurst's Royal Garage there were five others vying for the motorist's custom, including the Tampico Garage on Slyne Road which the owner John Bell named after a town he had visited on the east coast of Mexico.

Tourism

This busy scene at Crosshill featured on a card sent by a holidaymaker to Manchester in 1910. It gave rise to quite a lengthy message on the back (bottom right).

Crosshill Bolton-le-Sands

In the summer months the population of Bolton-le-Sands swelled with holiday visitors and excursionists. When the tourist coaches pulled up at the Blue Anchor for refreshments, as in this picture from 1905, they would be surrounded by children who helped fix the nosebags of the horses and would try to sell the passengers bunches of wild flowers or watercress for a few pennies.

'I shall not be very brown, for the sun has not been hot enough for that but I think B-le-S suits me as well as anywhere I have yet had a holiday. This is a very lively corner. All the coaches from Morecambe draw up to water the horses and on fine days dozens pass through on the way to Silverdale and Arnside. I am sorry my holidays are nearly over. I have enjoyed them so much. Kindest regards to all at home.'

Shoreside Bolton-le-Sands

At the end of St Michael's Lane were a number of cottages that put up visitors during the summer months. Edna, the writer of this card posted to Manchester in July 1919, was lodging with Mrs Cook at a house called Sandside: *'We are having a lovely time. It is a country place and very quiet, but the sea comes up and there is a proper beach but there is no promenade. The cross is the house where we are staying. I shall be brown as a berry soon.'*

Farms also took in holidaymakers as a means of supplementing their income. Mrs Shuttleworth of Bolton was the recipient of this card of Mill View Farm from her daughter in July 1924: *'This is the house where we are staying at and we are having fine weather and we have been to Morecambe today and it was lovely.'* Today, Mill View Farm is no longer a working farm, most of its land having been sold for housing and its outbuildings converted into residences.

Mill View Farm, Bolton-le-Sands.

This card of Waterside, almost opposite Sandside, was sent to Bolton in August 1912: 'We are having a lovely time. Bolton-le-Sands is a pretty place. Frank is enjoying himself and eating like a horse. He has had three eggs for breakfast this morning. By the way Doris, he was riding a horse yesterday and got thrown off. The water was very high yesterday, right up to the wall of our house.' The house was built in 1687 by William Hall and his wife Jennet, son and daughter-in-law of John and Jane Hall of Church Cottage.

Holiday lodgings were also available at several houses in the village, such as St Michael's Cottage next to Boys School Bridge. It was known as Bridge Cottage when this card was sent by a couple staying there in August 1946. Writing to a friend who was planning to join them, they had decided that Bridge Cottage had insufficient room and so were moving to Sandside near the shore: 'We are going into a little better home so we shall be able to accommodate you.' By the 1960s it was taking visitors under the more formal name of the Hill Croft Guest House but is now a private residence.

Maud posted this card of Ivy Bank House, Town End, to her father and sisters at Farnworth in August 1906: 'We arrived safely about half past six. This is our home and we are enjoying ourselves very much although it has rained all day. John has caught an eel.' Ivy Bank House belonged to poultry dealer George Mayman but it was his wife Elizabeth who looked after the guests. A similar card (with similar weather!) sent to Rochdale in July 1913 from Alf and Lizzie contained the message 'Just a line to let you know we are on our holidays staying at the house which is on the front. The weather is not what we would like it to be. There is a lovely view of Morecambe Bay here.'

Winding through the centre of Bolton-le-Sands the Lancaster Canal was a popular leisure facility for both visitors and locals. It was frequented by walkers, anglers and various sorts of craft which could ply the waterway as far as Tewitfield without the inconvenience of lock gates to negotiate. On this card from 1915 a couple in a rowing boat have the canal to themselves as they make their unhurried way towards Packet Bridge.

Exactly a century since the demise of the packet boats in 1846 a company called WATERWAYS inaugurated a passenger service between Hest Bank and Carnforth via Bolton-le-Sands. A number of old landing craft were obtained and renovated and seats fitted. The boats, with their green canvas canopies and names such as *Lady Ruth* and *Lady Pat*, proved an attraction for many years. Here two of the fleet can be seen passing under Town End Bridge.

CARD
Address.

Military

BOLTON-LE-SANDS
--- CAMP ---

In 1908 the Territorial Forces Act created a volunteer force, the forerunner of today's Territorial Army. As well as giving up some weekends, Territorial soldiers were required to go on an annual camp, usually of two weeks' duration, where they would do training exercises such as fitness marching, field manoeuvres, rifle shooting and perhaps, as on this card, learn to use a machine gun. Locations in north Lancashire and southern Cumbria were favoured by various Lancashire regiments and camps were held on a regular basis at Bolton-le-Sands, Caton, Halton, Hornby and Kirkby Lonsdale.

Here kilted soldiers of the Liverpool Scottish Regiment are pictured marching from Bolton-le-Sands station to their campsite. The sender of the card has identified himself with an X. Two weeks later the Scots struck camp and were replaced by, among others, units of the 4th Battalion King's Own Royal Regiment from Askam, Millom, Barrow, Dalton, Ulverston and Cark, part of an overall total of 2,500 officers and men – more than twice the population of the village at the time! After they left, the third and final camp of the year was filled by soldiers from south Lancashire and Cheshire.